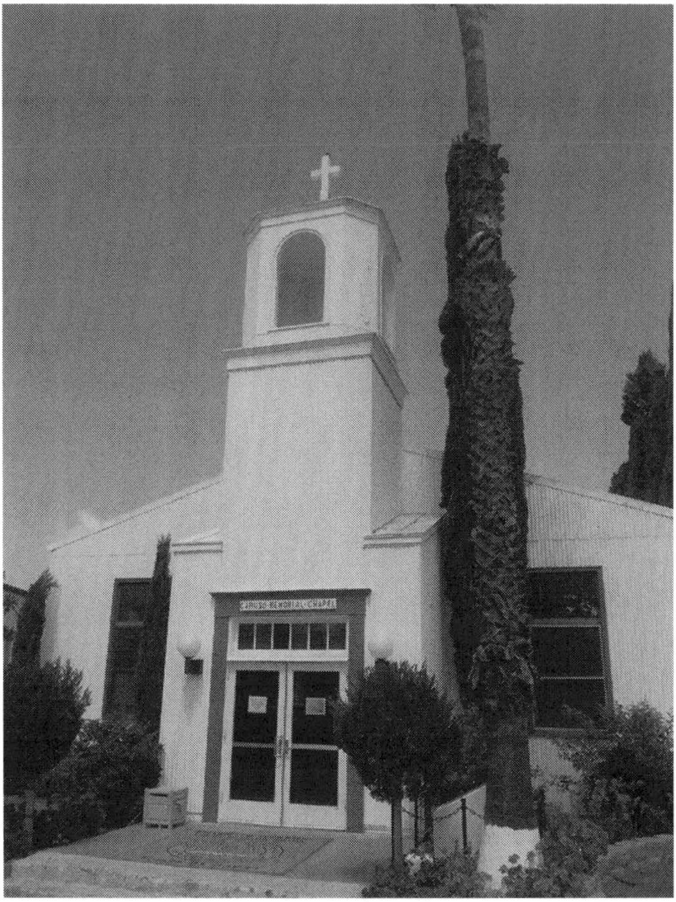

Semper Fi, Padre

The Mathew Caruso Story

By JOHN CARUSO and AARON ELSON

Published by:
Chi Chi Press

ISBN: 978-0-9969602-0-5
www.semperfi-padre.org

Chi Chi Press
"A Good Little Publishing Company"
New Britain, CT
888-711-8265

To Marilyn

About the Authors

John Caruso is a retired Superior Court judge, having spent one year hearing civil and criminal matters and 13 years in Family Court. He also is a Certified Public Accountant. He has returned to practice, handling Alternative Dispute Resolution matters as well as Estate Planning, Probate, Family and Business matters. He is a Marine Corps veteran of the Korean War and is very active in the Greater Hartford, Connecticut community as well as in the Avon, Conn., Veterans of Foreign Wars and a number of other organizations including the Farmington Chapter of UNICO and the Farmington Exchange Club. He lives in Avon with his wife, Marilyn, and his Golden Retriever and Maine Coon cat.

Aaron Elson has recorded more than 600 hours of interviews with veterans of World War II. He is the author of "Tanks for the Memories," a collection of stories told to him by veterans of the 712th Tank Battalion, with which his father served, and several other books. In 1997 he launched the World War II Oral History web site @ tankbooks.com. His work has been used as source material in more than two dozen books and a dozen documentaries, some of which have been shown on the History Channel. He is currently producing a series of Oral History Audiobooks, while working as a copy editor at the New Britain Herald. He lives in New York City.

Foreword

It was an iconic moment in an iconic battle, one of the fiercest in Marine Corps history. On the night of Dec. 6, 1950, during the breakout from the Chosin Reservoir, 19-year-old Sgt. Mathew Caruso, a chaplain's assistant, saved the life of Navy Lt. (j.g.) Cornelius "Connie" Griffin at the cost of his own life. Six days later, in Rocky Hill, Conn., Daniel Caruso, Mathew's son, was born. When Danny was 14 months old, he was given his father's posthumous Silver Star in a ceremony that made national headlines. In 1953, the Caruso Memorial Chapel was dedicated at Camp Pendleton. Sixty-three years later it's still a focal point of life at the sprawling Marine base.

Mathew Caruso was my brother. I followed him into the Marines, and caught the very end of the Korean War. When Mathew's remains were repatriated in 1955, I had the honor of being his burial escort by train from San Francisco to Hartford, where Father Griffin said the Mass at his funeral.

"Semper Fi, Padre" is the story of Mathew's sacrifice, and the ways in which a death in combat can have a profound effect on a multitude of lives.

— John Caruso

Mathew Caruso's Silver Star citation

"For conspicuous gallantry and intrepidity in action against the enemy, while serving with a Marine infantry regiment in Korea on 6 December 1950. Serving as assistant to the regimental chaplain, Sergeant Caruso displayed outstanding courage and devotion to duty when the convoy with which he and the chaplain were traveling in an ambulance was ambushed by a large enemy force employing intense and accurate automatic weapons and small arms fire. Quickly throwing the chaplain to the floor of the ambulance, he shielded him from the enemy with his own body, and in so doing was mortally wounded, gallantly giving his life for his country. Sergeant Caruso's heroic and self sacrificing actions were an inspiration to all members of the command, and were in keeping with the highest traditions of the United States Naval Service."

"Temporary Citation."

Contents

John Caruso at the 2014 rededication of the Caruso Memorial Chapel.
Marine Corps photo by Sgt. Christopher Duncan

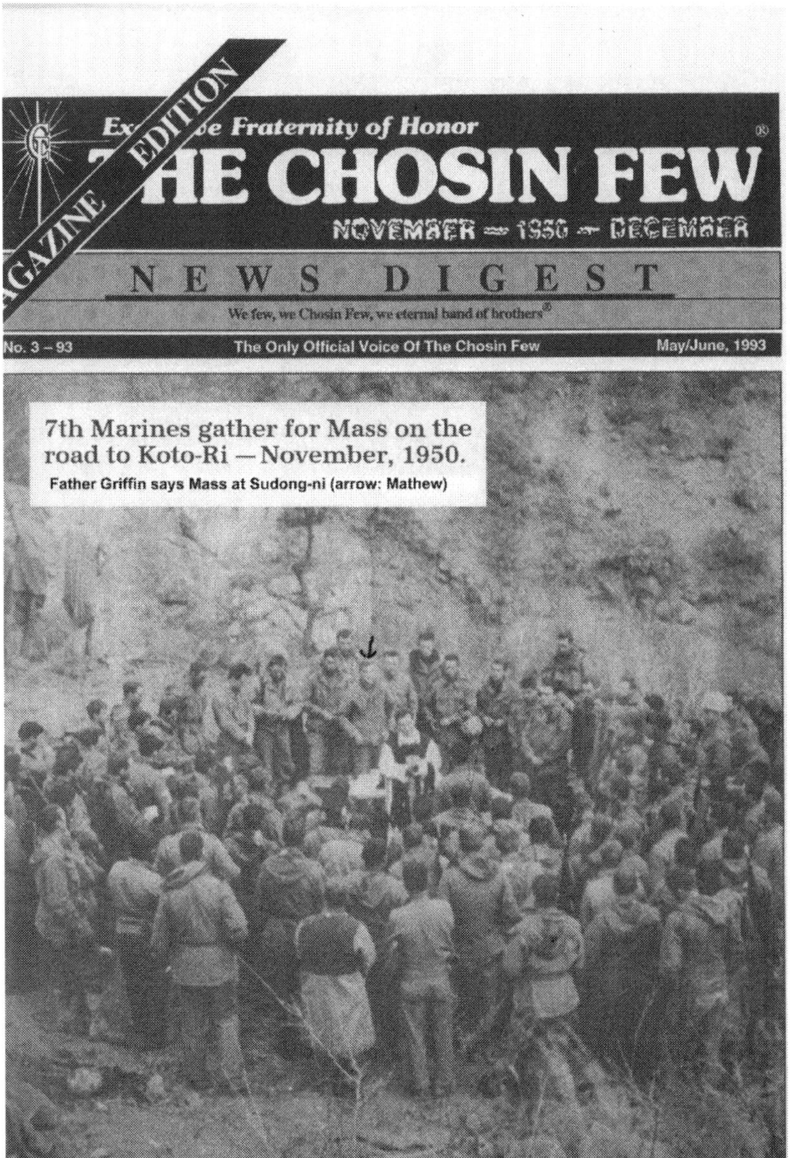

A 1993 cover of "The Chosin Few" showing Mathew and Father Griffin.

The entrance to the Caruso Memorial Chapel

What's in a Name?

In the north end of California's Marine Camp Pendleton stands the Caruso Memorial Chapel, built in 1953. It's just off Basilone Drive, which is named after World War II Medal of Honor recipient John Basilone. The chapel has been a focal point of life in the School of Infantry West, formerly known as Tent Camp 2, for more than 60 years. Although it is non-denominational, it's the only one of three chapels at Camp Pendleton that has a cross on the top. In the 1990s it fell into disrepair and there were rumors it would be torn down, but members of the Church of Latter Day Saints, which holds services there, took it upon themselves to refurbish the chapel and landscape the grounds.

"When I first became stationed here I thought to myself, what is the Caruso Memorial Chapel?" says Navy Lieutenant Commander Evan Adams, a Seventh Day Adventist. Adams took over as command chaplain at the School of Infantry West in April of 2013 following tours on the USS Chancellorsville and at the Naval Nuclear Power Training

Command. He served in Afghanistan, where he organized a program that delivered birthday cakes to Marines in the field, from March to October of 2010. "What does Caruso mean? Is that a person? Is that a place? Like some ships are named after people, like the USS Higgins [named after Marine Col. Richard Higgins, who was murdered by Iranian terrorists in 1990], and then some of them are named after places, like the ship I was on, the Chancellorsville, which is named after a Civil War battle. I wanted to know who Caruso was and what it meant.

"I started with the plaque out front. It was severely corroded. It was barely readable. In Naval tradition we have what's called the Jack of the Dust. The Jack of the Dust, his job is to shine the bell every morning. So I employed one of the volunteer Marines who work at the chapel. He goes out there every day and shines the brass, so that now it's readable. And about the third day I was here I began to learn who Sergeant Caruso was."

Incidentally, Caruso has more in common with Medal of Honor recipient Basilone than an intersection at Camp Pendleton and their Italian American heritage. Basilone had already been awarded the nation's highest military honor and was back in the States raising money for war bonds, but he felt his duty lay more with the men who were still fighting overseas and requested to be returned to the 1st Marine Division, which in 1944 was fighting in the Pacific. Basilone was killed on Iwo Jima in 1945. Mathew's wife was expecting their first child and his chaplain, Father Cornelius "Connie" Griffin, arranged for him to remain behind when the 1st Marines were sent north to the Chosin Reservoir, but Mathew, the chaplain's assistant, insisted on accompanying him into North Korea, feeling it was his duty.

Mathew Caruso was a brother, a husband, and a son. He was about to become a father. He was a happy go lucky, mischievous kid who ate french fries one at a time and never put ketchup on them, who didn't finish high school and enlisted in the Marines at the age of 17. He was good looking, athletic, loved to play baseball and liked to emulate his big brother Mike, who was a Navy corpsman on Iwo Jima during World War II.

Mathew was assigned as the assistant to Father Griffin during the early months of the Korean War. He was 19 years old.

"Suddenly a flare went up on the flanks; the red cross on the side of the ambulance offered a perfect target for some Red machine gunner; he blazed away — and the ambulance was riddled with bullets. Sergeant Mathew Caruso, who was helping Griff, anticipated the situation by a fraction of a second. Screaming 'DOWN!' he literally knocked the chaplain to the floor of the vehicle. In so doing, he saved Chaplain Griffin's life, at the sacrifice of his own; Caruso was dead when the firing stopped."

— Rev. John Craven, in "A Bullet for the Chaplain"

Coming Home

June 1, 1955 — It was raining. It seemed like it had always been raining, making everything damp and dreary. Or maybe it was just the mood I was in ever since I received my orders. They came as no surprise, for I knew they would be coming. I was about to complete a journey that began more than five years earlier in a cold, distant place far from home.

I looked out the window. The rain was coming down faster. I could see Marines, like so many soaked animals, scurrying for shelter.

It was late in the day. I glanced at the clock on the barracks wall. I changed into my dress uniform. It felt warm, and I began to sweat. I left the building, giving a nod to the guard on duty, and crossed the street. As I neared the large, gray, headquarters building, I began to feel tense. This was no time to start worrying, because there were many things that would be required of me. I shrugged, took off my cap, and entered.

I walked down a dimly lit corridor until I came to a door with "Escort Section" printed in bold, black letters. I knocked, opened the door, and stepped inside. A captain was sitting behind one of the few desks in the room, writing on some papers. He looked up and motioned to me to have a seat, then continued writing. After what seemed a long time, he looked up again and asked if I was ready to leave. I said I was. He reached into a drawer and removed a large manila envelope. He stood and handed it to me. I saluted, turned and exited.

I left Camp Pendleton for San Francisco by train the following morning. The sky was overcast, and the threat of more rain was in the air. I kept to myself, but it was difficult for a Marine in a Class A uniform with a black armband to maintain his anonymity. As I stood on the platform after the casket was loaded onto the train for the trip across country, a middle-aged woman approached and asked about the armband.

"I'm a burial escort, " I said, "for a fallen Marine."

"How did he die?" the woman asked. It was peacetime, after all.

"He was killed in the Korean War," I said. I didn't mention that he had been buried, along with some 60 other Marines and British commandos, in a mass grave in earth so frozen that dynamite and a bulldozer were needed to dig it, at a place called Koto-ri, or that he was repatriated from North Korea during Operation Glory, in which the remains of 1,500 soldiers and Marines and commandos were exchanged for the remains of several thousand North Korean and Communist Chinese soldiers killed south of the 38th Parallel.

"Where are you headed?" the woman asked.

"He's going to be buried in Hartford, Connecticut."

"Were you in Korea?"

"I was, but only at the end of the war."

The woman glanced once more at my black armband.

"Did you know him?"

There was a lump in my throat. "Yes," I said softly. "He was my brother."

In the Bible it says "Greater love hath no man than that he lay down his life for his friend." On Dec. 6, 1950, my brother, Marine Sgt. Mathew Caruso sacrificed his life to save the life of Navy chaplain Cornelius "Connie" Griffin. Mathew was 19 years old, although his Silver Star citation says he was 20.

The woman returned to her husband, and I could see her most likely telling him about me. Another passenger, I imagine having seen her conversing with me, joined them and probably asked about the armband.. By the time I boarded the train and made my way to the club car, it was no longer possible for me to buy a meal. It was impossible to buy a drink. It seemed everybody on the train wanted to know about my mission and my brother.

In 2009 I saw the movie "Taking Chance," in which Kevin Bacon portrays Marine Lt. Col. Michael Strobl, who is the burial escort for a Marine killed in the first Gulf War. Even though his journey was by plane and mine was by train, it brought back many memories of that trip and inspired me to write this book.

Mathew's death has been described in several books about the Chosin Reservoir. But those books, studded as they are with deeds of heroism, don't go into the far reaching effect Mathew's death — like the deaths of so many young men and women in combat — had on so many lives, not the least of which has been my own.

My father, Michael Caruso Sr., was wracked with guilt because he allowed Mathew to enlist when he was 17, a year after our mother's death. Mathew was the fifth of ten children, two girls and eight boys. I was the seventh, with a sister born between Mathew and me. Two of our older brothers, Mike and Pat, both World War II veterans, went to a local tavern the night the telegram came and by closing time were ready to reenlist. They didn't — Mike already had two children, including a son born the day Mathew was killed. I joined the Marines and not only served in Korea as a communications specialist but had the honor of serving as my brother's burial escort.

Mathew's widow, Betty, gave birth to their son, Daniel, six days after Mathew was killed, and a week before the telegram announcing his death arrived. She remarried a veteran of the Chosin Reservoir campaign and had two daughters in addition to Dan.

Dan Caruso grew up to become a Marine helicopter rescue pilot. His cousin Larry, who was born the day Mathew was killed, retired as a sergeant major in the Marines. The chaplain whose life Mathew saved, Cornelius Griffin, went on to become a monsignor in the Tucson, Arizona diocese.

For more than 64 years Marines at Camp Pendleton have worshiped at the Caruso Chapel, named in honor of my brother, before deploying to the world's danger zones, and where chaplain Evan Adams makes sure my brother's story is told to every new group of recruits.

In 2014, Bulkeley High School in Hartford, which Mathew attended for three years, awarded him a posthumous diploma as well as a cap and gown, which I was able to present to his 83-year-old widow at a ceremony marking the rededication of the chapel later in the year.

This is Mathew's story.

"Having a Wonderful Time"

"Hello Dad," Mathew wrote in a letter from Camp Lejeune dated April 28, 1949, about a year after he enlisted in the Marines. "I have some spare time, so I thought I would write you and let you know how I have been getting along. I'm in the best of health and hope that everyone at home is the same. As for the weather, it has been very beautiful here for the past week, but since last night all it has done is rain ... rain ... rain.

"Dad, I'm sorry I didn't have the time to see you before I started back. I was at my girl's house in Rocky Hill most of the day and later on in the evening I was unable to get a bus back to Hartford. I stayed overnight at her folks and in the morning her mother drove me back. You weren't home, so I had to catch the train right away. Bud [our older brother Mike] and Annabelle gave me a ride to the R.R. Station and from there it took me 22 hours of riding to get back.

"Since arriving back at the base, our outfit has been on the move most of the time getting prepared to leave for Europe. The Chaplain and I [Mathew was already a chaplain's clerk, but had not yet been assigned to Father Griffin] have got all our office and personal equipment packed and ready to leave. Tomorrow we will leave.

"In the morning we will board a troop train and be on our way to Norfolk, Va. There we will embark aboard the ships that will take us across on our long voyage. There are two cruisers, the Juneau and Fargo, the aircraft carrier Coral Sea, and three LSTs. They are splitting up the men and putting them on all the ships. The Chaplain and I will go aboard the Coral Sea and what a swell ship she is.

"We are due to arrive at Gibraltar on or about May eleventh and relieve the outfit that is now over there. For a period of five months we will cruise all the Mediterranean area, and have liberty in a lot of places. Places like Casablanca, Tripoli, Libya, Athens ... Greece, Crete, Malta, Sicily, Rome, Naples, the French Riviera, and maybe even have time to go to Paris and Palestine.

"All in all, I think it will be very interesting and I'll remember a lot of things over in Europe. I'm going to see the Pope while we are in Rome and buy some souvenirs. If you remember any of your relatives over there [our father came from Castelfranco in Italy, and rumor had it we were distantly related to the great tenor Enrico Caruso] you could tell me just about where they live and I could try and see them.

"By the way pop, how is everything going along at home and how are you coming along with the house? Write and let me know how the kids are getting along, and don't forget to take care of yourself.

"Well that is about all I can say for now, but I will write soon. Tell Mrs. Sisson that I said 'hello' and I sure would like to have the [Hartford] 'Times' sent to me. Take care pop, write real soon and give my love to all.

"Love, your son, Matt."

There were ten children in the Caruso family — my family — eight boys and two girls. Mathew was the fifth and I was the seventh, with my sister Teresa in between. Mike, the third oldest behind George and Lucille, was a Navy corpsman during World War II and took part in the battle of Iwo Jima. Pat, the fourth oldest, served on the USS Midway. Our mother died in 1947 and our father was rarely home, so Mike was like a second father to Mathew. Although he'd been in the Navy, as a corpsman, which is the Navy term for medic, most of Mike's time was spent with the Marines, so it's little wonder Mathew wanted to enlist in the Corps. Our father objected to him enlisting at 17 but he eventually relented. World War II was over and while the Cold War was in its early stages, there was no reason to believe a shooting war was about to begin. Mathew got married while on leave and planned to complete his education when he got out of the service so he could get a better job and support his family. He was due to be released in August of 1950, but the Korean War broke out in June and his enlistment was frozen.

The war had not yet started, however, when he boarded the Coral Sea. Indeed, the itinerary, which was among Mathew's memorabilia, reads like that of a pleasure cruise. "Out at Sea," on 12 May, 1949, it begins. In May the ports of call include Gibraltar; Agusta Bay and Palermo, Sicily; June includes visits to Naples, Genoa and Rapola in Italy; July saw liberty calls in Gulfe Juane, France; Argostoli and Athens, Greece, and Istanbul in Turkey. August included stops at the island of Lemnos, Turkey; Crete and Naples; and the ship returned to Gulfe Juan and Gibraltar before putting out to sea once again and reaching Norfolk on Sept. 27.

Wide-eyed 18-year-old that he was, Mathew sent postcards from several ports.

"Hello Folks," he wrote to Mike and Annabelle on a postcard featuring a picture of Naples at night. "Mailing you this card from the Post Office in Naples. Having a wonderful time, and wish you could be here. Our fleet is anchored right in the Bay just like the picture on the reverse side. Take care, and I will write soon. Love, Matt."

On a postcard with scenes of the Cote d'Azur postmarked July 6 and sent from the Coral Sea, Matt wrote, "Hi Folks. Writing you this card from city of Cannes on the famous 'French Riviera.' The scenic beauty here is marvelous and have enjoyed liberty here very much. Already I have taken a lot of pictures and gone in swimming a couple of times. Will write soon and tell you all about it. As for now, take care, Love, Matt."

On a postcard with a picture of Istanbul and dated 30 July 49, Mathew wrote, "Hi Folks, Mailing you this card from the U.S.O. in Istanbul, Turkey. We are a long way from home but still manage to have a good time. Right now I'm on liberty with a couple of school chums from back home. Will write soon and tell you all about it. Take care, and see you soon. Love, Mickey."

Mickey was my brother Mike's nickname when he was in the service, although I remember his nickname more as having been Bud. Our father, a home builder and carpenter, was rarely at home, and whether Mike liked it or not, Mathew latched onto him as a kind of surrogate father.

"I'll tell you, Mathew was one good looking guy," Mike's widow, Annabelle, who's 83, recalled recently. "He was more of the non-Italian type. He had blond hair. I have a cute little story about him. He used to use the name Mickey when he was in high school, and my husband's name was Michael, but he went by the name of Mickey also. And the phone would ring, Mike would answer. 'Is Mickey there?'

"'This is Mickey.'

"And then he'd find out that it was for Mathew. And he also found out that Mathew was wearing his clothes. This was the thing that bothered him more than anything because my husband could come home drunk and he would stand in front of the closet, weaving back and forth, taking his clothes off and folding them and hanging them up."

After they were married, Mathew's wife, Betty, worked for a few more weeks and then quit her job in the stenography pool at the Travelers Insurance Company in Hartford so she could go and stay with Mathew in North Carolina.

They found what she remembered many years later as a tiny apartment in a shack that was converted into two apartments in the back yard of a home. "It was just a bedroom, a little tiny kitchen and a bathroom," Betty recalled, "and there was another apartment as well, plus the family had a couple living in their house."

The way Mathew described the apartment in a letter to Mike, you'd think it was a palace: "I found a beautiful little apartment we could live in right outside of the Camp, and then on the last of June she came down to North Carolina to live with me. It had three rooms and a bath and it was an ideal spot for the two of us."

The Forgotten War

Sandwiched as it was between World War II – the "Good War" – and Vietnam – the first war to be brought into our living rooms via television, the Korean War is often called the "Forgotten War."

The Korean War, however, was a veritable smorgasbord of diplomatic history, full of behind the scenes machinations by some of the most important names of the era: Josef Stalin, Mao Zedong, President Harry S. Truman, General Douglas MacArthur. With the Cold War in its infancy, the Korean War was the first major confrontation between Democracy and Communism.

Japan had colonized and occupied Korea from 1902 until the end of World War II. There might have been no divided Korea if, on the very day the atomic bomb was dropped on Hiroshima, August 8, 1945, the Soviet Union had not declared war on Japan. Prior to that, the Soviets and Japanese were technically not enemies. But by declaring war just a few days before the Japanese surrender, Stalin gained the right to a Soviet zone in Korea, just as Germany was divided between East and West. The Soviet and American zones of Korea were divided by the 38th Parallel.

Like some of the Middle East conflicts of today, the two Koreas fought what might be called a proxy war, as the Soviet Union and China jockeyed to expand their sphere of influence in East Asia and the United States implemented a foreign policy aimed at containing the spread of communism. By 1948, South Korea was led by a virulently anti-communist, albeit democratically elected, president, Syngman Rhee, while Stalin installed Kim Il-sung, the grandfather of today's dictator, Kim Jong-un, as the leader of North Korea. Both Rhee and Kim wanted to unify Korea, but it soon became apparent that there was no hope of unifying the two Koreas by peaceful means.

Stalin armed the North Koreans with tanks and heavy weapons, but in the late 1940s disapproved of North Korea invading the south, not wanting to risk a confrontation with the United States, which kept troops in South Korea. Meanwhile, there were numerous skirmishes as both sides probed the 38th Parallel, the majority of them instigated by Rhee, with thousands of casualties even before the Korean War began.

According to some accounts, the United States pulled most of its troops out of South Korea so as not to encourage Rhee, who was confident of U.S. backing, to invade the North. Then, on June 25, 1950, some 75,000 North Korean soldiers invaded South Korea. Within days Truman committed the United States to South Korea's defense and sought the formation of a multinational force from the United Nations. Ironically, the Soviet Union, which could have vetoed a Security Council resolution, had pulled its envoy some months before over the UN's refusal to seat China following Mao's defeat of the Chinese Nationalists, who had been pushed back to Taiwan.

The initial invasion by the North was highly successful. Seoul was captured within days and the small American force along with the Republic of Korea troops were pushed back to a 150-mile perimeter around the southern port of Pusan.

In a letter to Mathew, our older brother Mike refers to General MacArthur as "Dugout Doug," an appellation coined by his own troops on Corregidor in the early days of America's involvement in World War II. It was a reference to the feeling that he spent most of the battle in an underground complex in Corregidor and then abandoned the troops to direct the war from Australia, while many of the men left behind would be doomed to take part in the Bataan death march. Although some accounts contradict the image of MacArthur's reluctance to abandon the bunker, the nickname stuck, and dogged him throughout a distinguished career.

The great New York Daily News sports cartoonist Bill Gallo, whenever there was an important baseball or football game, would draw a caricature of the game's hero, accompanied by a caricature of its goat.

In the Korean War, MacArthur was both the hero and the goat. After the North Koreans invaded the South, captured Seoul and pushed the defenders to the Pusan Perimeter, MacArthur orchestrated the landings at Inchon, attacking the North Koreans from behind. This led to the recapture of Seoul and caused the North Korean army, cut off from supplies and replacements, to flee back to the North after heavy fighting.

The Inchon landings were considered a masterpiece of strategy. Just as MacArthur's decision to invade North Korea — ignoring the possibility of Chinese intervention in the war despite evidence of a massive buildup of troops along the border — was considered one of the greatest strategic blunders in history.

The 1st Marine Division, which included my brother Mathew and Father Griffin, took part in the landing at Inchon.

The Korean War, incidentally, was the first conflict in which units were integrated, with African-American and white soldiers fighting side by side, rather than in segregated units as was the case in World War II. And the Korean War gave us Radar, not the kind that was so important in World War II and later in controlling air traffic, but the bespectacled, diminutive character played by Gary Burghoff, along with Hawkeye Pierce, Trapper John and Hot Lips Houlihan in M*A*S*H*, the 1971 Academy Award-nominated movie (it was beat out for Best Picture by "Patton") and popular TV series, which probably did more to introduce the American public to the Korean War than anything else.

"The Happiest Fellow in the World"

In a letter to our older brother Mike written on Oct. 19, 1950, prior to the Wonsan landing, Mathew described the events of the previous weeks.

"Hello Mike," the letter, typed on Marine Corps stationery, begins. "Just a few lines to let you know where I am at and what I've been doing recently. I'm in the best of health and hope that you and everyone else at home is in the same. I realize that quite a bit of time has passed since I last wrote to you and I do deserve a good swift kick in the seat of my pants for not keeping in contact with the old gang. However, my only hope is that you will answer this letter as soon as you possibly can and let me know how you are and how everything is back in Hartford.

"Most likely you and a lot of other people were surprised when you found out that I got married. I'm sorry for not inviting you or any of my old friends to the wedding like I promised, but it was only a small affair and we were married just as soon as I came back from Division maneuvers in the Spring. I did marry Betty Russell and since that time I have been the happiest fellow in the world. She really is sweet-wonderful-considerate-kind, and loving and I knew that no one will ever be her equal. She is a wonderful wife Mike, and I really am proud of her.

"We were married in Rocky Hill and after the wedding ceremony we left by train to New York for our honeymoon. We planned on going to Maine for seven days but seeing as how my leave was only for ten days we couldn't go. While in New York we spent a wonderful honeymoon and the two of us were very happy. We had a bridal suite at the Hotel Taft in Times Square, saw all the sights, took in some Broadway musical shows, went to the ball game at Yankee Stadium and etc. After staying there for a week, we went back to Conn. and from there I had to go back to Camp Lejeune.

"Just as soon as I arrived back at the base, I found a beautiful little apartment we could live in right outside of the Camp. She stayed working at the Travelers for a couple of months and then on the last of June she came down to North Carolina to live with me. I had three rooms and a bath and it was an ideal spot for the two of us. I didn't want her to work because believe it or not, I found out that she was going to have a baby. Everything was going really swell for the both of us when suddenly everything that I thought would never occur did.

"On the 11th of August the entire 2nd Marine Division left the East Coast by troop train for Camp Pendleton in California. I hated to leave because everything was wonderful in our little home and we did find all the happiness in the world. Our good-bye had to be quick and I then sent her back home to Rocky Hill to stay with her folks until I did come back. It took us five days to go from North Carolina by troop train to California. While in California we underwent some very rugged training and received many lectures on various weapons, terrain in Korea, and etc. I thought we would stay on the West Coast for a while, but we were there only eleven days when we were told we're moving out.

"On the 28th of August our regiment (changed from the old 6th Marines to the 7th Marines, 1st Marine Division) left the United States. After spending 19 days aboard a troop transport we arrived at Kobe, Japan on the 16th of September. From what we were told, we were going to receive advanced training before going to Korea. However, the very next day we left Japan and soon thereafter landed on the beaches of Inchon, Korea. Our landing was behind the enemy lines and our objective was the South Korean capital of Seoul. The Marines along with the 7th Army did take Seoul, but it was a rough and bloody battle taking the place. I was there the day General MacArthur came in. However, we didn't stay there very long because the Commies were on the run and we had to chase them. We then traveled and fought our way from Seoul to the city of Uijongbu which is located only a few miles from the unforgettable 38th Parallel. We took up defensive positions there and stayed there until we were relieved from the front lines by the Republic of Korea troops and the 1st Cavalry Division.

"We then went back to Inchon-Korea where we had made our initial landing. During our time there we re-organized and were issued new clothing, equipment, weapons, and etc. On Sunday the 8th of October a beautiful Memorial Service was held at the 10th Corps cemetery for our fallen comrades who had been killed in action. Our casualties were just about 6,000 men, six hundred of whom are lying under those white crosses back on that hill in Korea. A lot of them were some of my closest friends and I'm never going to forget them. They all gave their lives fighting for what is right and my only hope is that this war is over soon and there will be no more bloodshed.

"I'm still working for the Chaplain only this time I'm working for a Catholic priest. He really is a wonderful guy and the best guy I have ever worked for. He's the one in the middle of the picture. He's done everything for his boys and I've never seen such a heroic guy in my entire life. One day while we were fighting for Seoul, I saw him give Holy Communion and the last rites on his stomach while under enemy machine gun and sniper fire. Every day he has Mass for the men and he's really a nice guy to have around.

"Working for him is okay and I don't mind it at all. I still do all the administrative and clerical work that needs to be done, also write letters of condolence to the loved ones of the fellows that have been killed, help and aid the wounded men at aid stations, and also am his bodyguard and serve Mass with him. I go to Mass whenever I can and have received Holy Communion quite frequently. There were also many times that we said the Rosary together at night in our foxhole and believe me it's done a lot of good. I know that God is watching over me and, if I put my faith in him, I'm sure he will want me to come back from all this.

"Right now the 1st Marine Division is back aboard troop ships and are sailing somewhere along the East Coast of North Korea. Our schedule calls for us to land at Wonsan tomorrow morning and our objective is the capital of Pyongyang. MacArthur is going to start his big push real soon and I believe that our outfit will be in on it. Most likely we will be committed to action sometime in the early part of next week. I think it will all be over soon because they are on the run and after their capital falls I think they'll surrender. Many of us are hoping and praying that it will be over soon, because none of us like fighting this war or any part of it.

"My wife is going to have a baby pretty soon and then I really will be happy and my life will have been made complete. She really is wonderful Mike, and I do love her an awful lot. It certainly is going to be nice when I can hold her in my arms once again and be able to pick up our baby too. When I do get back to California after this is all over I'm going to have her and our baby come out to California to live with me. I'm sure they'll like it very much and the climate really is wonderful.

"I was supposed to get discharged this coming February but now I won't get out until the early part of 1952. I'll have a little over four years in then and probably add another stripe to my sleeve. Not only am I held over for an extra year but also the same goes for Bob, Dick and Cinc. It is an involuntary extension and I really don't mind it at all. If I was a civilian when this war started, undoubtedly I would have been drafted or enlisted.

"I know that Richie Le Clair is back in and so is Billy Ulich, and Ed Connors. In fact the entire Marine Corps Reserve is now on active duty. We had only one Marine Division when this started but I can guarantee you there'll be plenty more divisions before this is all over. I also read in the papers where the Connecticut National Guard was called to active duty. I was wondering if Bill O'Brien and Nelson and those fellows left. Maybe you have already been drafted yourself or perhaps you may have joined up. Write and let me know when the fellows are being called and what your intentions are. O.K.?

"I know that Dick is over here somewhere but I don't know what ship he is on. Also Gene is somewhere around here because he was on Guam when this war did start. If you have their addresses, I would appreciate it greatly if you could send them to me.

"I've enclosed a picture which we had taken at Inchon just before we went back aboard ship last Saturday. Father Griffin is in the middle of the picture and if you are wondering why he is armed, he has a good reason. They have already killed a Catholic priest over here and wounded two other chaplains from our Division. Maybe that other fellow in the picture looks like a crazy guy, but he's one of the bravest most heroic guys I know. He's been recommended for the Bronze Star for carrying wounded Marines back to the Aid Station when they were pinned down under enemy fire. He also is in the chaplains section, only he works for a Protestant Chaplain. If you ever get the chance, Mike, I'd like you to show the picture to a couple of the priests at Saint Augustine's. They might know Father Griffin.

"Right now I'm earning $205 a month and almost all of the money is being put into the bank by Betty. She is under a good doctor's care at home and her mom and dad really have done everything for the two of us. With the money I have when I return to the States, I have intentions of building our own home somewhere in Connecticut. As yet we haven't got the G.I. Bill of Rights but I think we are going to get it pretty soon. I'm the type of guy that will take advantage of some of the benefits too.

"Write and let me know how everything back home is and how your folks are. Tell them I said hello and also tell 'Minerva' I was asking for her. And, if you see any of my old friends tell them I was asking for them. When you do write let me know how the high school and college football games are going and about the latest fights. I'd also appreciate it greatly if you could send a couple of pictures too. What I really would like is a couple of prints of the pictures we had taken Easter Sunday of '46. O.K.?

"Maybe I won't get back home for a long time to come, but I want you to know that when I do, I'll be sure to see all of my old buddies and friends once again. I still haven't forgotten the party we planned on when all of us fellows get out either.

"Well, I'll have to be securing this letter for now as they will darken ship in a few minutes. Don't forget to write and send the pictures. Take care of yourself Mike, write soon, and I am hoping to see you someday again real soon.

"Your old buddy, Matt."

That "other fellow" in the picture was James Engeldinger, who, like Mathew, enlisted in the Marines at 17, although Engeldinger would one day admit to having lied about his age. He later served in Vietnam with the 9th Infantry Division, and retired as a major. He was awarded a Silver Star in Vietnam, along with two Purple Hearts. I don't know or don't remember many of the names referenced in Mathew's letter, but they were from Hartford and if they or any of their relatives wind up reading this I'd be happy to hear from them.

I don't know if there was an earlier letter from Mike to Matt, but considering the time it took for letters to travel it's likely his letter dated November 26, 1950, which follows, was in response to Mathew's letter of October 19. Mike's letter was marked "Return to Sender" with a postmark of Jan. 2, 1951, almost a month after Mathew was killed.

"Dear Matthew," Mike's letter begins [he spelled Mathew's name with two t's, a common mistake]. "Hope this letter finds you O.K. I know it is pretty rough where you are at this writing. Well, I will give you the news up to date since I last heard from you.

"To begin with, you never sent me your address so how could anybody write to you? The last I heard was that you were on your way to Camp Pendleton and you did not give me your address after that.

"Dad has received 2 letters from you so far. According to the date that they were mailed, it takes about two and a half weeks for mail to get to the States. And so I got your address from one of the letters.

"At the present time everyone at home is okay. About 2 months ago Dad fell off the scaffold up at the house in Bloomfield. I took him to the hospital. He broke his back in 2 places, broke 3 ribs, tore the ligaments in his shoulder and fractured his right arm. He was on the critical list for 4 days and was in St. Francis Hospital for 5 weeks. He is in a plaster cast from his neck down to his hips right now, but he is at home and on the mend. It will take time for it to heal but he is tough. He even drives the car now but he can't work yet. He will have to have the cast on for a couple of more months.

"Your picture was on the front page of the Hartford Courant 2 weeks ago. Your chaplain, two Gyrenes and a Chinese monk and it said that you were just north of Wonsan at the time it was taken. I sent to the Associated Press and they sent me the original. I gave the picture to Dad and he was proud to see you on the front page.

"Dad sold the house in Bloomfield to Bill Lee, the Sports Editor of the Hartford Courant. Mrs. Sisson is in the hospital for an operation and she is coming along alright.

"Bill and Pete are still as frisky as ever and they got a big kick out of seeing your picture in the paper. Billy lost a tooth.

"Ralph got honorable mention at Bulkeley High and is doing well in his studies. But he is still very lazy.

"John got a new .22 rifle and has more hobbies than you can think of. He gave up his paper route and is now working for Schuster at the Five and Ten in Barry Square. He supports Ralph.

"Pat is working nights now at Underwood and was thinking of going back in the service. He asked me to go in with him.

"George and Pat were up to see us tonight. George is working in a shop in Torrington and he has a 1947 Buick now. He and Pat went to the Ice Capades in New Haven tonight.

"Well, Theresa [the sister born between Mathew and me] is now living with us. She has a job at Loew's Poli selling candy. Dad gave me an extra room, so we made it into a living room and Theresa sleeps on the sofa-bed.

"As for my own family, we are expecting an addition any moment. Carol is 13 months old today and you should see her. She was walking at 8 months and she even talks a little. She must have known I was writing about her because she just woke up. We are hoping the baby will be a boy. It is due this week.

"We haven't heard from Betty but we hope that she is doing fine. Hope she and the baby will be happy. Don't worry about it. All the Caruso's are tough.

"When I get some pictures taken of Dad & the kids I will send them to you. According to 'Dugout Doug' [Douglas MacArthur], you'll be home by Christmas. I hope so. I know what it is over there.

"Now I'll tell you the odds and ends since you left. I saw O'Brien about 3 months ago and at that time he was still down South. I saw Mrs. Gasner's grandson and he is also in the Marines at Camp Lejeune. Annabelle's cousin joined the Marines last week. The draft is scooping them in around here. Aunt Julie passed away 2 months ago and was buried in Tarrytown. I was sorry to hear it but I couldn't go to the funeral.

"Well, we have a new governor, John Davis Lodge. Bowles got beat. Bulkeley High School just went through their first undefeated, untied football season. They had a good team. Of course you know my Yankees won the World Series, and Notre Dame has had a so-so season. There is a new heavyweight fighter who has created a sensation, a white ex-GI by the name of Rex Gayne.

"Harold Houle, your old friend, got arrested for taking a motor vehicle without permission. I was elected 1st Vice Commander of the

Catholic War Vets post and we are fighting for the Korean Vets to receive the same benefits that we got. Without a doubt you'll get them.

"Pat's, mine and your name will be together on the honor roll at St. Augustine's. Captain Oakley was asking for you.

"Carol fell down a week ago and we took her to the hospital. She had X-rays taken and is okay now, but she had a nice lump on her head.

"Junior Johnson got married in Dobbs Ferry last week. Aunt Rose and Uncle Rocky were up to see Dad and they were asking for you.

"We had a hurricane here yesterday and last night. The house leaked all over. I had to climb on the roof to get a hatch cover that blew off. Connecticut got hit pretty hard, in fact all of the Eastern states were. Pittsburgh and Cleveland were paralyzed and Hartford had a state of emergency. Wind was up to 100 miles an hour. I imagine it's pretty cool where you are. How would you like to take a dip in the Changjin Reservoir? Br-rr.

"I'm still drawing on the side.

"Glad to hear that you are working for a Catholic chaplain now. So will Saint Sebastian. Incidentally he looks like a pretty good Joe.

"If I could afford it, I would have sent you a Christmas present but due to insufficient funds I couldn't.

"And if those rotten 'Chink Reds' don't drag back into their own territory I'm afraid Pat and I will go. Hope it gets over soon and you will be on your way to a happy family life.

"Will write you again as soon as I get some pictures to send along. Try to take care of yourself and stick close to the Chaplain. Everybody sends their love and be real assured that everything in the States is okay.

"Brother Bud."

I always thought Mike didn't attend Mathew and Betty's wedding because they didn't get married in a Catholic church, but according to Mathew's letter to Mike they got married without telling our family.

As for the "hurricane," it was actually a rare "Southeaster" that roared in from the Appalachians, instead of the usual nor'easter that comes up the coast. It hit Hartford with sustained winds of 70 miles per hour and gusts of up to 100. And the "addition" to their family that Mike and his wife, Annabelle, were expecting is my nephew Larry, who was born on December 6, 1950, the very day Mathew was killed.

When Mike wrote that the Carusos are tough, he wasn't kidding. When my father fell off that scaffold, it was because the scaffold was improperly set. He stepped on the edge of the scaffold, there was nothing there to hold it, and his weight was enough to flip it. He was heading right for a big piece of concrete, and he was falling head first. So he did a somersault and landed on his back. He probably would have been killed if he landed on his head. But he was very strong and athletic, and the doctor told him if it had been a man who was not in as good physical shape as he was, he would have been dead. He even trained for the 1912 Olympics but according my grandmother wouldn't let him go to Sweden because she didn't want him to be tempted by all those Swedish blondes. And he was on board ship to go overseas to fight in World War I when the armistice was signed. But getting back to the accident, he was too stubborn to call an ambulance, so he drove himself home. Only he couldn't shift gears with his broken right arm. My little brother Billy, who was 5, was with him, so Dad told him to move the gearshift while he operated the clutch, and the two of them made it home. When Mike arrived a short time later, he immediately called an ambulance.

We Carusos were not only tough but we were good looking as well. I knew very little about my father's first wife other than that she was George's mother and she died during the global influenza pandemic of 1918. I only recently learned from my oldest sister Lucille's daughter that Dad's first wife was a Ziegfield Follies girl.

From my father's obituary in the Hartford Courant: "He was a well-known builder in the area, having built many custom homes and commercial buildings. He was superintendent of construction of Constitution Plaza, the Travelers Insurance Cos. and the Hartford Insurance Group. He was a former Connecticut amateur featherweight and bantamweight boxing champion. He had played football for the Meriden West Ends. In 1912 he finished seventh in the Boston Marathon. He was a candidate with Jim Thorpe for the U.S. Olympic team in 1912."

Betty Caruso Smith *(Marine Corps photo by Sgt. Christopher Duncan)*

"I'm Never Going to See Him Again"

On June 26, 1950, on the outskirts of Camp Lejeune, North Carolina, Mathew and Betty Caruso were sharing their first few weeks of living together. After they were married, the young couple had stayed with Betty's parents in Rocky Hill, Conn., while Mathew waited to complete his enlistment. That enlistment was frozen when the war broke out.

A major and his wife "lived in the next little apartment," 83-year-old Betty Smith — Mathew's widow — recalled during the 2014 rededication of the Caruso Memorial Chapel at Camp Pendleton, "and the major brought Matt home one night so he could say goodbye to me." Betty was pregnant, and had lived with her husband for less than six weeks.

"I was totally shocked," she said. "I have no idea how I got home" to Rocky Hill, "but when I got there my father met me and I said, 'I'm never going to see him again.'

"And my grandfather, my mother's father, said to my mother, 'I hope she hurries up and has that baby before she gets bad news.'"

Mathew's unit, the 7th Regiment of the 1st Marine Division, was sent to Camp Pendleton in California prior to deploying to Japan and then Korea, and he was reassigned from Father Patrick Killeen to Father Griffin. Several years later, quite by happenstance, I met Father Killeen at Camp Pendleton, where he told me how he wound up giving the last rites to a badly wounded Father Griffin as well as to my brother at Koto-ri.

Cornelius "Connie" Griffin was born in Indianapolis in 1920. He enlisted in the Navy and was himself a chaplain's assistant in World War II. After the war he attended the Pontifical College Josephinum in Worthington, Ohio.

According to a newspaper article, he was the youngest chaplain ever commissioned in the Navy when he received his lieutenant's bars.

Father Griffin "donned the bars of a lieutenant junior grade 10 months after he entered the priesthood," the article said. "Currently, clergymen entering U.S. military service 'must have five years experience' before receiving a commission, Griffin quipped. 'I don't know if I was the cause of this rule being instituted.'"

On Aug. 12, 1950, Griffin received orders to report to Camp Lejeune for overseas duty.

"The activities of a chaplain are many and varied. But before he can be of practical aid to the men under his charge, he must get their confidence," Griffin told the Josephinum Review during a 1951 interview.

He knew from his earlier service "that the best indication a chaplain has that he has gained the confidence of his men is by the name they call him," the article said. "When the stiff term 'Chaplain' changes to a cheery 'Father,' then he knows he's 'in.'

"Father Griffin went about getting 'in' with the men from the very beginning of his assignment with the regiment. The trip from Virginia to California took the 7th Marine Regiment a week. This was the getting acquainted period for the padre. He heard confessions and otherwise spent his time talking with the men. All knew that many of their number would not return. This might be their last opportunity to talk to a priest."

When Griffin arrived at Camp Pendleton, Mathew was assigned as his assistant. As there was no place to hold services, Mathew set up a makeshift chapel in a Quonset hut in Tent City 2. It is near this site that three years later a permanent chapel would be built in his honor.

Mathew, left, and Father Griffin in Korea

Inchon

Barely a month after arriving at Camp Pendleton, the 7th Marines took part in the landing at Inchon, north of Seoul. The South Korean capital had been captured in a lightning strike by the North Korean army in an attempt to unify the two Koreas by force, and the defending United Nations troops were pushed back to the Pusan perimeter on the southeastern tip of the Korean peninsula. The landing at Inchon, coupled with the Army approaching from west of Seoul in a pincer movement, threatened to cut off the invading North Koreans from their ability to be resupplied and reinforced, and they fled back across the 38th Parallel before they could be completely enveloped.

Mathew and Father Griffin waded ashore at Inchon on Sept. 21, 1950.

"Working his way down a rope ladder into an invasion boat was a brand new experience for the padre," the 1951 article in the Josephinum Review said. "Under cover of darkness, the invading group hit the beach and immediately pushed inland. Late that night the battalion was two and a half miles behind enemy lines — a place they did not want to be. The situation was remedied without a single casualty. By the time the proper rendezvous was reached and a comfortable foxhole dug, the chaplain was ready to rest. He had been carrying a full field transport on his back, a .45 on his hip, a Mass kit in his right hand, and another leather grip with ecclesiastical supplies in his left. The nine and a half miles of hiking and evading the enemy had been a little more than he had bargained for.

"For the next nine days, the Marines were held in reserve at Inchon. Griffin was able to say Mass in relatively peaceful surroundings, and some 450 Americans killed in the battle were buried. Griffin had comforted many of them in their last moments."

Encouraged by the success of the Inchon landings and the liberation of Seoul, General Douglas MacArthur, the supreme commander of the Allied forces, ordered a second amphibious invasion, this time on the eastern shore of North Korea. After several ships were damaged or sunk by mines, the landing at Wonsan took place on Oct. 26. Ironically, because of the delay so the mines could be cleared, the Army captured Wonsan before the first Marine came ashore, and Bob Hope came, performed for the troops, and left a day before Mathew arrived.

The landing was uncontested, but it could have turned tragic.

"Father Griffin is a stocky fellow of thirty," the Josephinum Review wrote in its 1951 profile. "During his days in the seminary he was referred to as a member of the 'beef trust.' No one was surprised that he should mention his padding when he told about his experience at Wonsan.

"The invasion boats could approach only to a certain point offshore. The remaining distance had to be waded. There were 300 yards of water between the landing group and the shore. The water came above the hips of most of the men. The temperature was 21 degrees above zero. A chilling rain was falling.

"'Sergeant Mathew Caruso nearly froze to death,' relates Father Griffin. 'He didn't have the blubber to protect him as I did.'"

In all likelihood the war would have been over with the liberation of Seoul, and America, which provided the largest contingent of the United Nations forces, would have been hailed as the hero if the UN troops had stopped after forcing the North Korean army back across the 38th Parallel. But MacArthur, ignoring reports of a massive buildup of Communist Chinese troops along China's border with North Korea, decided to pursue the North Koreans all the way up to the Yalu River, the Chosin Reservoir, and the border with Manchuria.

John Craven, the regimental chaplain of the 7th Regiment and a close friend of Father Griffin, didn't mince words in a 1980 oral history. Craven, a Baptist who served as a chaplain in World War II on Kwajalein, Saipan, Tinian and Iwo Jima, noted that his feelings about the Korean War contrasted with the official policy, especially the views of General MacArthur.

"While we were in South Korea," he said, "the men felt that they were on a crusade. They would come to me and say, 'Chaplain, we are really helping these people out. The communists came in and took over their country and their homes and we are driving out the enemy and we are restoring their homes to them.' But the very minute the word got around that we were going into North Korea everyone was going around with a sick feeling down in the middle of his stomach. We would go because we were ordered to go but there wasn't any of this sense of a crusade."

By the end of September 1950, Craven said, "all of the North Korean forces had been defeated and Seoul had been restored to the Korean government. If we had stopped right there we could have said to the world, 'You see what happens when you try to use aggression or force to put over your ideas?' Psychologically we would have been in a tremendous position, but the very minute we started talking about going across the 38th Parallel into North Korea then the whole situation switched. ... To me military force is in order to stop aggression and for defense when you're attacked, when freedom is threatened. Somebody was trying to use force, and we stopped the aggression very quickly."

U. S. Marines talk with Brother Pincentius, O.S.B., acting Brother Superior of St. Benedict's Monastery, North Korea. From left are: T/Sgt. Robert W. Arsenault; Sgt. Robert J. Pachucki; Brother Pincentius; Lt. (JG) (Chaplain) Cornelius Griffin; and Sgt. Matthew Caruso. Father Griffin said Mass in the destroyed monastery.

The Tokwan Abbey

After landing at Wonsan, Mathew witnessed firsthand the devastation wrought by the North Koreans on the Catholic church.

According to "The History of the Navy Chaplain Corps," the 7th Regiment's three chaplains, John H. Craven, Father Griffin and Kester M. Hearn, "spent several nights in a burned-out Benedictine Abbey in Tokwan, about eight miles north of Wonsan.

"The three chaplains settled down in the Abbey's undamaged school building, and in the chapel each conducted religious services. Chaplain Griffin, a Roman Catholic, was greeted with joy by many of the natives who said that he was the first priest they had seen for over a year.

"Later Chaplain Griffin, [in a 1951 interview], commented on the enthusiastic reception given to him by the Roman Catholic Koreans at Tokwan. He said: 'The reception by the people was unbelievable. They fell all over me when they learned I was a priest and begged me to come and celebrate Mass. Several hours afterwards I did — my first High Mass in the Navy.'"

More than 500 villagers attended the Mass. Marine Lt. George Balzer and Brother Pincentius, a Korean, "led a hastily assembled choir of more than 100 in the Gregorian music of the Mass," according to the Chaplain Corps history. "'Nothing ever sounded more beautiful to me,' Father Griffin said. 'Practically everybody there received Communion.'

"Here the Marines were seeing at firsthand some of the evidences of the way the Communists were persecuting the Christians," the history continued. "They learned how the Communists, when they retreated from the Wonsan area in the first part of October, had spread straw through the beautiful Abbey church, poured on gasoline and set it afire."

At the Tokwan monastery, Mathew and Father Griffin posed for a picture with two other Marines and Brother Pincentius, who was one of only three Benedictine monks who remained. Most of the monks had been taken away by the North Koreans, and the monastery's abbot, Bishop Boniface Sauer, died in a North Korean prison camp in February of 1950. (In 2007, Bishop Sauer was proposed for beatification, along with 35 other Benedictine monks from the Tokwan monastery who either were executed or died in prison camps. The case is still pending.)

The 7th Regiment's respite at Wonsan was to be all too brief. "MacArthur's planners had called for United Nations forces to push forward to the Manchurian border, securing North Korea in a three-pronged drive to the Yalu River," the 7th Regiment's official history says. "Units of the 1st Division were ordered forward to occupy the Chosin and Fusen Reservoirs. Other elements were dispersed over 300 miles to link with Allied units. Intelligence reports stated that North Korean forces were on the run, disorganized and would offer only token resistance. ... Maybe, the reports speculated, the Chinese or Russians would intervene, but there was no hard evidence.

"The reports of the North Korean capabilities were gravely underestimated, and the speculation on potential Chinese involvement was flawed. Determined and organized North Korean attacks were initiated against a battalion of the 1st Marines at the coastal town of Kojo, south of Wonsan, on October 27. Outflanked, outgunned, and faced with well coordinated night attacks on their positions, the Marines called in close air support and artillery.

"Two days later, when the action was broken, as the enemy withdrew into the mountains, prisoners revealed that the Marines had been attacked by three battalions of one of the best units in the North Korean army. And there were still up to 7,000 North Koreans in the area."

If the Inchon landing was one of Douglas MacArthur's greatest victories, the decision to cross the 38th Parallel and pursue the North Koreans to the border with China proved to be his biggest blunder.

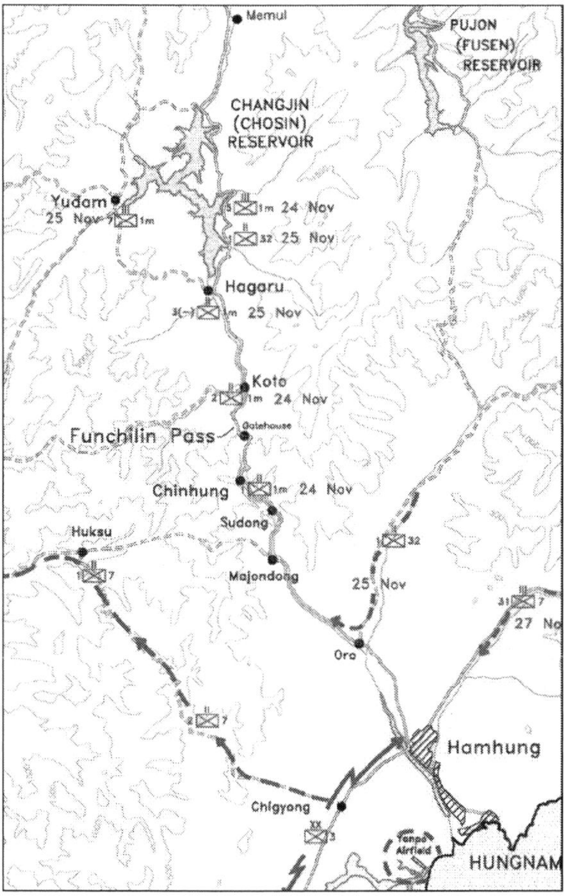

A Bugle Calling Whistle Blowing Attack

The 7th Marine Regiment (Mathew's unit) was the first American outfit to go head to head with the Chinese, on November 3, 1950, during what the regimental history called "a midnight bugle calling and whistle blowing frontal attack near Sudong."

"The 7th Marines ... spearheaded the thrust northward from Hamhung toward Chinhung-ni, about 35 miles distant," the Chaplain Corps history says. "On the night of 2-3 November this advance force engaged a full Chinese Communist division. ... Thus the 7th Marines had the distinction of being the first American unit to be engaged with a Chinese Communist force in large-scale combat. A furious five-day battle followed, during which the enemy's casualties were estimated to have run as high as 9,000 with over 660 killed. The Marine casualties included 46 dead and 264 wounded.

"During the battle, two battalions of the 7th Marines were attacked from the front and on both flanks for about 24 hours. With these two battalions were Chaplains Griffin and Kester M. Hearn. Here Chaplain Griffin so distinguished himself that he was recommended for and later received the Silver Star."

Stanley Modrak, an 85-year-old Marine veteran living in San Francisco, was severely wounded in the battle. He passed out from loss of blood after three machine gun bullets struck him in the side and forearm, and came to briefly ... just as Father Griffin was giving him the last rites. He passed out again and came to in a field hospital.

Modrak, who would suffer from post traumatic stress disorder, described the incident in a memoir titled "Hostage of the Mind — a Korean War Marine's Saga of War's Trauma and the Battle That Followed Him Home."

"As each November nears and northern California's blue skies and wind-blown clouds flee, surrendering to a glowering, gray overcast, I recall a bleak fall of 1950 in North Korea," Modrak wrote. "Disquiet memories intrude; discordant bugles blaring, echoing from hill to hill high above; sudden shock and fear as fingers of death clutch; a shadowy figure hovering."

The 1st Marine Division was marching toward the Taebaek Plateau, which led to the Chosin Reservoir, Modrak wrote. "The ultimate goal was to traverse the desolate Taebaek Mountains, secure the Chosin Reservoir, then continue northwest over the mountainous spine of North Korea to eventually link up with the U.S. 8th Army driving up the western side of the Korean Peninsula. Col. Lewis 'Chesty' Puller's 1st Marine Regiment along with Lt. Col. Ray Murray's 5th Marines would follow. After a day-long trek climbing a narrow single-lane dirt road rising northwest, Col. [Homer] Litzenberg chose a small, rock-strewn valley just south of a North Korean hamlet called Sudong-ni to bivouac his regiment for the night."

Sudong-ni means "town by the river," Modrak said recently by phone from a hospital bed in California, where he was recovering from heart problems.

From his memoir: "During chow line with evening approaching fast, we heard scuttlebutt rumors that Red Chinese troops had been contacted nearby by Republic of Korea units. Actually the ROK's 26th Regiment that we were replacing had indeed run into Chinese soldiers, taking 16 prisoners. The Red Chinese were clad in quilted uniforms, mustard color on one side and winter white on the reverse side. They wore fur-lined caps with ear flaps and most had canvas shoes with crepe soles that our Marines called tennis shoes — we couldn't understand the shoes in the North Korean winter."

Colonel Litzenberg, Modrak wrote, once said "The only Marines I want in my outfit are Purple Heart Marines."

"As the crisp, darkening night air found the 7th Marines breaking out sleeping bags and preparing to sleep," his book continues, strains of 'Goodnight Irene' filtered through our bivouac area" via Armed Forces Radio Tokyo. "Meanwhile, unknown to the slumbering Marines, the Red Chinese 124th Infantry Division of General Sung's 42nd Field Army poised its 186th and 187th Regiments to hit Marine hill positions in a classic military double envelopment."

"A double envelopment is usually pretty damn deadly," Modrak said during our phone conversation. To make matters worse, he added, General Sung told his Red Chinese troops, "Kill these Marines as you would kill snakes in your homes."

Despite decades of PTSD, Modrak noted in his book with a sense of Marine pride that "those snakes delivered a powerful bite."

At 11:30 p.m., Modrak was awakened by cries of "Here they come!"

"We scrambled from our sleeping bags arming ourselves with M1 carbines and .45s," he wrote. "A blare of discordant bugles echoed eerily from hill to hill above. Soon shadowy forms rose from the murky darkness in the river bed to our left. As we let go with a fusillade of weaponry the forms faded into the deepening gloom. ... I marveled at the guts of our battalion officers as they stood tall in the valley's center, directing their Marines' defenses even though parachute flares exploding overhead bathed the tiny valley in a ghostly yellowish aura.

"As mountain rivulets unleashed by a spring thaw form, multiply and then rush downhill following paths of least resistance, so too came the Red Chinese. Breaking past and veering around strong points, relentless bands of quilt-garbed Chinese infantry cascaded into, through and around Leatherneck hill positions intent on swarming into the valley floor battalion command posts."

As the battle raged, Modrak and his radio team were positioned to cover the riverbed when a non-commissioned officer shouted "One of you, come with me!"

"Marine discipline kicked in," he wrote, and he ran with the officer for 50 or 60 yards "that seemed like a hundred" as tracers lit up the night and the sound of gunfire was all around. "Miraculously" making it through the gauntlet of fire, Modrak "dove into the shadows behind a low stone wall."

When the burst of three machine gun bullets struck, "slamming into my side and forearm," he wrote, "sound, feeling, disbelief all jumbled together in a disjointed sensation as I realized I was hit."

He tried to shout "Corpsman!" but could only produce a murmur. "Marines nearby took up the call as I slumped to the rocky earth. With consciousness rapidly fading, Colonel Litzenberg's words, 'Only Marines ... my outfit ... Purple Heart,' were my last thoughts.

"Reviving sometime later in the still smothering darkness, I sensed a shadowy form hovering over me. Was it an enemy, a fellow Marine, or...? Quiet, firmly enunciated words broke the chill night air: *'In nomine, Patris, et Filii, et Spiritus, Sancti, amen.'* I then realized that the form must be our regimental chaplain, Father 'Connie' Griffin, pronouncing the Last Rites of the Catholic Church. Growing up through twelve years of Catholic schooling I knew full well their dire implications. 'Am I dying, Father?' I murmured. Passing out once again, I never heard any response. Awakening the next morning to daylight in a medical tent with other litter-bound wounded, it sure felt reassuring to be still among the living — also, there was no significant pain in my side that took two of the three rounds. Relief was short-lived, however. Crack! Crack! Dirt began kicking up in the tent's dirt floor only a few feet from my litter! What a helpless feeling that was not knowing where the next shot would hit. 'Sniper!' yelled a corpsman. They began putting helmets on the litter-bound wounded to hopefully provide some sort of protection as the intermittent firing continued. Being half out of it, I don't know if the Chaplain was in our med tent while the sniping was going on. Foolishly, our Navy surgeon opened the tent's flap to look outside. Crack! 'Ugh'

He bent over in pain as a slug tore into his thigh. Soon the fire ceased as we learned that Fox Company was busy clearing the snipers from a nearby hill."

By the end of the battle at Sudong-ni, Modrak wrote, "General Sung's 124th Infantry Division was rendered ineffective and withdrawn from action for the war's balance. With another heroic victorious chapter added to the Marine Corps' illustrious history, Colonel Litzenberg's 7th Marine regiment began to resupply and prepare to resume their drive to the Chosin Reservoir."

Although his name is not in any of the accounts at this point, Mathew never was far from Father Griffin at Sudong-ni.

Joseph Quick, a veteran of Okinawa in World War II and the 7th Regiment at the Chosin Reservoir, also described an encounter with Father Griffin in a 2010 interview with Don Moore for the Veterans History Project.

"I was hit in the butt, back and legs by shrapnel from an enemy mortar," said Quick, of Port Charlotte, Fla. "The only thing I remember is leaving the ground when the incoming round hit.

"When I woke up I was in a blacked-out tent in a rear area with the dead, the dying and the wounded. I couldn't see anything, but I could hear a Catholic chaplain giving a Marine his last rites.

"A few minutes later the chaplain crawled over to me.

"'Father, I'm not a Catholic, I'm a Baptist,' I told him.

"'Son, do you believe in God?' he asked.

"'Yes sir,' I said.

"'Let's say a prayer together,' the priest suggested.

"I lay there praying in the dark with the chaplain.

"After he left, I said an extra little prayer of my own. I told God, 'If you'll get me out of here alive, I'll never use your name in vain again.' To this day, 54 years later, I haven't. That's pretty damn good considering how salty a Marine's language can be."

"For conspicuous gallantry and intrepidity as Chaplain for the Second Battalion, Seventh Marines, First Marine Division," Griffin's Silver Star citation begins, "in action against enemy aggressor forces in Korea from 2 to 8 November 1950. During the height of a fierce, coordinated night attack conducted by the enemy against elements of the Seventh Marines, Chaplain Griffin repeatedly exposed himself to heavy hostile fire as he moved among the troops giving encouragement. Later, when the same units of his battalion were subjected to heavy small arms fire, he left the comparative security of the sick bay and moved back to the front lines where he again braved hostile fire to render aid and comfort to the men wounded in the attack."

"Father Griffin ... was a young priest right out of the seminary. At first he had been taken aback by the profanities and vulgarities that were the prevalent language of his flock of Marines. He adapted quickly, though, and ... had the reputation of showing up when there was a firefight going on." **–Joseph Owen, in his book "Colder Than Hell"**

"Home by Christmas"

"Before Thanksgiving," the 7th Regiment history says, "the 1st Marine Division and other United Nations forces were ordered forward to the vicinity of the North Korean and Manchurian borders bounded by the Yalu River. ... A bitter, sub-freezing winter had set in, glazing the roadway with ice, freezing streams, and layering the ground with hard-crusted snow.

"Engineers improved the road, installed culverts and plans were made for a 5,000-foot airstrip at Hagaru-ri. Air-dropped supplies could satisfy some, but not all, of the needs.

"MacArthur ordered the advance to the Yalu for November 24, and units of the 1st Division moved north on the west side of the Chosin Reservoir through fields of snow."

In his book "Colder Than Hell: A Marine Rifle Company at Chosin Reservoir," Joseph Owen talks about the regiment's chaplains.

"The men asked Reverend Craven if it was true that we were going up to the Yalu, and after that, whether it was true that we would be home by Christmas," he wrote.

"'It's straight dope that we're headed due north and right up to the Chinese border,' Reverend Craven told the men. "But only the Lord knows about getting you boys home by Christmas. That's the best I can tell you.'

"'Father Griffin, the Catholic chaplain, was a young priest right out of the seminary. At first he had been taken aback by the profanities and vulgarities that were the prevalent language of his flock of Marines. He adapted quickly, though, and, like Reverend Craven, he had the reputation of showing up when there was a firefight going on. During the lulls, when he came up to us, he always said Mass for the troops, and he insisted that Joe Kurcaba and I attend. Before Mass he heard confessions and advertised himself to the troops as 'the easiest confessor in the history of Catholicism.'

"The troops checked with Father Griffin to confirm that we were headed north to the Yalu, as they had with Reverend Craven. And whether we were going home for Christmas.

"'Colonel Litzenberg himself told me that our objective is the Yalu River,' the young priest would answer. 'But I don't know whether God has made up His mind yet when we're going home.'

"To the men in the rifle companies, the 'word' wasn't straight dope until the padres said so."

"MacArthur was very optimistic about what was happening," Craven said in his oral history. "He kept talking about being home by Christmas. He and other military people kept talking about the North Koreans, saying, 'The Chinese communists will not dare to come in. This is all bluff, this is all propaganda.' But when our regiment — we were the point regiment out of Hamhung going into North Korea and we hadn't been up there very long — ran smack dab into the Chinese communist division in 'Nightmare Alley,' I saw Chinese communist soldiers with their quilted uniforms piled up in ditches six deep all around where our regiment had stopped them. We ran into all kinds of them and they kept trying to break through with their bugles blowing and human waves coming oon. That's the way they operated in the beginning, but that was just very shortly after we got out of Hamhung and started north. They just kept pouring more and more at us and we kept meeting more and more of them all the time, but we just kept marching north in obedience to orders.

"That 'Nightmare Alley' was a tremendous nightmare as far as the chaplains were concerned because of the number of casualties we were receiving and bringing into the aid station."

From the regimental history: "First contact came on November 27, between elements of the 5th Marines and Chinese forces. On the 25th, Chinese forces had thrown massed assaults against the U.S. 8th Army and the X Corps, and II Republic of Korea Corps who were also advancing on the Yalu. Massed Chinese assaults cut the Marines' main supply route [MSR], separating the 5th and 7th Regiments [Mathew's] from the rest of the division. The 8th Army was by now in retreat, and the two isolated regiments were threatened with being overrun."

By November 28, the history says, "there was no one echoing the phrase repeated during the landing at Wonsan: 'We'll be home by Christmas.'"

In two days, it adds, the Marines suffered 1,094 casualties, including 871 killed, wounded or missing. The rest were lost to frostbite. And eight Chinese divisions, some 80,000 men, "were massed along a 25-mile front."

"The very minute we started talking about a landing in North Korea and how we were going to get the enemy and began advancing into their territory, then we were doing the same thing that they did when they crossed the 38th Parallel and went into South Korea," Craven said in his oral history. "and of course militarily it was very controversial. When the First Marine Division — the one we were with — was ordered to go into Hamhung and up to the Chosin Reservoir into North Korea, the G-4 of our Division wrote a statement of over 20 pages explaining why a Marine division is not equipped and suited for going over all of this land. A Marine division is equipped for an amphibious operation and the equipment and the vehicles and everything you have is for that purpose; and for us to start over so much land was to many of us a complete misuse of a Marine division. ...

"We should never have gone north of the parallel," Craven said in his oral history. "We gave all the psychological advantage to the enemy, to the communist forces. ... That foray into North Korea to me was one of the greatest mistakes militarily that America made after responding so tremendously and getting the United Nations' support and support from British and Turkish troops. When we started to go into North Korea to take over and to make them do things by military force, then we switched the whole thing and the Chinese communists came in by the thousands and that's what we ran into."

"Dear Pop, Please don't worry about me," Mathew wrote in what likely was his last letter home, "for I am taking good care of myself. I am confident that someday I will come back to all of you. I have an awful lot to live for — there will be my wife and baby waiting for me when I get back to the States. Of course I can't tell how long it will be before we are home again, but I do know that I will be one of the many guys aboard the ship heading back home when it is all over.

"I have enclosed a couple of pictures taken by a photographer at Inchon just before we left for here. I wish you would send me one of yourself, for the only ones I have of you and the family are in my album back home.

"I still am working for a chaplain, only this time it is a Catholic priest I am with. ... Every day when it is possible he says Mass for his boys and I have seen him give Holy Communion and administer the last rites under heavy machine gun fire by the enemy."

Johnny Carson: It was so cold outside ...
Audience: How cold was it?
Johnny: It was so cold, the politicians had their hands in their own pockets.

The Frozen Chosin

How cold was it at the Chosin Reservoir?

"The temperature was from minus 20 degrees to minus 40 degrees," veteran Don Dugay of the 1st Marine Engineer Battalion wrote in a diary, describing the trek from Wonsan to Hagaru-ri. Escerpts of the diary were published by the Korean War Veterans Association in 2005. "My best buddy and I had to start all the vehicles every one-half to one hour and let them run for about 15 minutes to keep them from freezing. At about 3 hours and 45 minutes I told Melton Brock I couldn't take any more, my feet were frozen and painful. He told me to go to our pup tent, he would finish the watch. He came in about 10 minutes later crying from the pain. I took off his boots for him. It was really cold.

"Capt. Turner had Brock and me inspect a bridge on the way to the Yalu River, to see if it was capable of holding trucks and tanks. On the way back we heard an incoming shell. We both dived into a hole made by another shell. Brock tried to climb out of the hole when another shell came in. The concussion knocked him back in. It was funny, because he was all arms and legs. That's when we found out the Chinese had us surrounded.

"On the way back to our CP, Brock was in front on my left about twenty yards. I saw an Army guy I thought was dead. I thought I heard a cough and went back to him to find he was alive, but exhausted and freezing. I pulled him up and half carried him for about two miles to our CP. I brought him to sick bay but he was in pretty good shape by that time. He was disoriented and would have frozen or been killed by the Chinese if I didn't hear him.

"Capt. Turner said seeing as I found him I was to spend the night with him in my foxhole. That's when he told me he wanted to stay with us Marines. He was angry at the Army for running and leaving him."

Temperatures in November and December "ranged from above freezing to 35 degrees below zero," according to a 1st Division special action report published online by the Korean War Project. "During this action the Division encountered both wet-cold and dry-cold conditions."

The terrain, the report noted, was mountainous, with "one main road which marked the route of advance and for a time was used as the MSR. Much of the road was tortuous, narrow and ice and snow coated."

Often C rations froze, and were partially heated at best, adding diarrhea to frostbite as a serious problem among the Marines. Water froze in canteens and men had to subsist on the snow which was in plentiful supply.

"During the day," Duguay wrote in his diary, "we worked on building an airfield to evacuate wounded. Sometimes we carried ammo up to the infantry. On one occasion I saw a radio man about halfway up. He said he couldn't go any further. I offered to carry his radio, about 60 or 70 pounds. When we got on top of the hill, I was talking to two guys when what I thought was a dead Chinese fired his burp gun at us. Hit the two on either side of me but not, or at least I thought, me. I carried one of the guys down.

"Whenever we carried ammo up, we carried wounded down. I noticed my mitten had blood in it, but I thought it was blood from the guy I brought down. I took care of the wound myself. The corpsmen and doctors were busy enough. Besides, I wouldn't want my parents to get a telegram and worry. I wish I had the Purple Heart now.

"Spent a night with a British Marine — swapped emblems. I still have his, but forgot his name.

"Another night was with Nick from Arkansas. He said for me to stay awake the first 100 percent alert. If the enemy came, to start shooting; if they got too close, wake him. As if an M1 going off in his ear wouldn't wake him up. During his turn to watch while I slept, or tried to, I heard him shoot. I and the guys in holes on either side of us asked him what he was shooting at. He said he was test firing to see if his rifle was frozen.

"Another guy, Corporal Hicks, needed to urinate. He asked if I had a grenade tube or box. I took off one end and put the grenade on top of the foxhole. He took off the other end, leaving a tube. He put his finger in the tube to let him know when to empty it. His parka was soaked and quickly froze. It was funny for me, but not for him.

"One night the Chinese attacked the airfield — we fought them off.

"One morning an old Papa-san came out of his house to urinate. A guy in the next hole from me fired his M1 at his penis and was laughing. I aimed my rifle at him and said his next shot would be his last.

"Frozen C-rations is all I remember. The only things I salvaged from the box of rations were cigarettes, powdered chocolate and Charms candy. For thirst we took handfuls of snow.

"One day I went to the old man's house, a couple of hundred yards away, and gave him and his family C-rations I didn't like or wasn't able to eat because they were frozen. The old man gave me a pipe, which I still have. I had to take it, although I didn't want to. They didn't have many possessions.

"Comes the time to defecate, I had three pairs of pants on. To unbutton you had to remove your mitten, and unbutton about two or three. Put the mitten back on and wait until your fingers were warm enough to continue. Total about fifteen buttons. Then reverse procedure. About an hour. Talk about freezing your butt off."

Johnny Carson: Last night it was so cold ...
Ed McMahon: How cold was it?
Johnny: It was so cold the flashers in New York were only describing themselves.

The Mother (Nature) of All Battles

On Nov. 10, 1950, the 7th Regiment of the 1st Marine Division occupied the Koto-ri plateau, according to "A Brief History of Dog Company, 2nd Battalion, 7th Marines." Coincidentally, it was the 185th anniversary of the birth of the Marine Corps. The events to come, however, would be anything but a piece of cake.

"This first night on the plateau would see the 7th Marines' new enemy, Mother Nature," the company history says. "In the afternoon and night the temperatures dropped to minus 8 degrees with winds 30 to 40 miles per hour. As D Company reached the positions it would occupy the first night, it began to snow. Foxholes were dug and by dark, the Marines settled in for the frigid night. The effect on the men was severe, with many collapsing. Nearly all became disoriented and respiratory problems became epidemic. One such Marine, whose running nose collected in a sizable ice cube in his newly formed mustache, cried in agony. Heat and stimulants had to be used."

(Speaking of stimulants, one story I was told by a veteran of the Chosin Reservoir was that Father Griffin would go from foxhole to foxhole distributing holy water to the frigid and weary Marines. This "holy water," the veteran said, was between 80 and 100 proof.)

"The next three weeks would see the weather become colder, but would not impact the troops as severely as the first onset of freezing temperatures as the Marines became acclimated to the temperatures," the Dog Company history continues. "Mother Nature did not side with either the Chinese or the UN forces, but exacted a heavy toll on both."

By November 15, "Mother Nature had rendered ineffective" about 200 Marines of the 1st Division with illness and frostbite, the company history says. "Other problems plagued the troops because of the freezing temperatures. Canteens had to be carried inside the clothing and the C-rations froze. When frozen or partially frozen rations were eaten it resulted in severe intestinal problems. As a result the troops ate only the dry portions of the rations, which resulted in dehydration and lowered calorie intake, and as a result the troops at Chosin lost an average of 20 pounds during the engagement. The cold had an adverse effect on weapons, ammunition and equipment as well. The government gun lubricant proved to be too heavy, resulting in malfunction of most weapons. The troops found that Vaseline and Wildroot hair oil was a great substitute when a thin coat was applied. The artillery pieces became sluggish, and the atmospheric conditions shortened the range. The reservoir received its Marine name, the 'Frozen Chosin.'

"The cold weather gear also proved to be unsuitable. The cold weather boots that were issued proved almost immediately to be inadequate. The Shoe-Pac consisted of a rubber foot, leather top and felt insoles. During marches the feet would perspire in the boots, and when one stopped the water would freeze and result in frostbite. It was necessary to change socks and insoles numerous times a day. During contact with hostile forces there wasn't time to change socks and insoles, and as a result many Marines suffered severe frostbite resulting in amputation of fingers, hands, toes and feet."

The day before Thanksgiving, "D Company moved out from Hagaru-ri and by mid-afternoon reached and took up positions on the ridge some 300 to 400 yards west from Toktong Pass. The night was bitterly cold ... but peaceful. The traditional Thanksgiving dinner was served on the road on the reverse slope of the ridge; however, it became a race to see if it could be eaten while still warm and before it froze. Fresh fruit, oranges or apples, didn't help the intestinal problems suffered by many Marines.

"Thanksgiving Day was cold and snowy, but all troops, except 1st Battalion 7th, were treated to the traditional roasted turkey dinner with all the trimmings.

"Contact was made by elements of the 1st Battalion with Chinese troops in the valley leading into Yudam-ni. With artillery and air support the Chinese were driven off."

After the Thanksgiving dinner, Father Griffin told his mess sergeant to take the red cellophane that the turkeys came wrapped in, and to use it to wrap up all the bones he could find.

"My God," the sergeant said. "What do you want with that junk?"

"When we get up farther north," Griffin said, "if we have to, we can boil the hell out of those bones in melted snow and make some damned good turkey broth."

Which they did later in the week. But Griffin wasn't finished with the cellophane wrapping.

"We reused it a second time to cover all the holes and loose corners in the sick bays during blackouts," he said in "The Korean War: An Oral History," by Donald Knox.

On the night of Nov. 27-28, "bugle-blowing, screaming Communists began to attack at Yudam-ni," the Navy Chaplain Corps history says, "and it was soon apparent that they were present in overwhelming numbers. Shortly afterwards enemy forces, deployed along the thin supply line which connected the advance body of Marines with its base at Hamhung, began to cut the main supply route in several places. The temperature was dipping to subzero readings during the nights. Little wonder that many were nearing the edge of nervous exhaustion, not far enough gone in battle fatigue to warrant hospitalization, but giving clear signs of bone-weariness: wan face, trembling hands. 'Shook,' they would say of such a one; 'he is shook.' Dietary deficiencies were beginning to appear because of the lack of hot food, and many of the Marines were suffering from diarrhea. Weapons often froze to such a degree they were rendered unserviceable."

In "A Bullet for the Chaplain," a story about Mathew's sacrifice first published in 1953, Reverend Craven relates a story about a Marine who was "shook":

"'Can you spare a few minutes, Chaplain?'

"The voice came from a bulky figure a few feet away in the darkness. It was muffled, but there was no mistaking the note of urgency it carried.

"'Of course! What's up?'

"'There's some wounded over there in that shack ...' The soldier pointed through the gloom, and 100 yards or so distant I could make out the dim silhouette of an abandoned Korean house. 'The doctors haven't been able to get to 'em; don't know when they'll make it. You might be able to help some.'

"'I'll sure try!' I'd carried a first-aid kit ever since this death march began and, whenever possible, I gave the medics a hand. When I got to the Korean house I found three wounded Marines stacked like logs on a pile of sawdust in the back. I knelt down, put my hand on the shoulder of one big lad, and started to speak:

"'This is Chaplain Craven, son. Can I do anything for you ...?'

"In a fraction of a second the big fellow knocked me violently to one side. The next thing I knew, I was staring fascinated at his upraised right hand, which grasped a long, wicked Marine trench knife! There was no question at all about what he intended to do with it; he was bent upon plunging it in my heart!

"One of his buddies grabbed the big fellow and pulled him back down. 'You'll have to forgive him, sir,' he apologized. 'He must be out of his head!'

"'There's nothing to forgive, son,' I assured the second chap quickly. 'It's combat fatigue; the man's nerves have snapped.'"

"We had what was called in World War I 'shell shock,'" Craven said in his oral history, recorded in 1973. "In World War II they called it 'combat fatigue,' but out in Korea we just said they 'got shook.' Some of these cases we dealt with, and sometimes the doctor would turn them over to me and say, 'Chaplain, you take care of these psychological casualties.'

"I remember one night we were taking a lot of casualties," he said of the incident described in his story, "and we had a little Korean house that the doctors were using the treat the wounded, and the doctor said, 'Chaplain, we have some men out there that are shook up. How about seeing what you can do with them?'

"There were about ten or twelve men who had been brought into the aid station but they weren't wounded physically. The first one I started to stoop down and say something to went berserk, grabbed his K-bar knife and started at me. I saw it coming in the dark, but I grabbed his arm and the knife just barely scraped my hand. We got hold of him and calmed him down, but we did a lot of work with these cases.

"Men went to pieces — they were shrieking and crying, gritting their teeth and jumping every time a shell would go off or land nearby, not being physically wounded but just psychologically shaken up.

"The most effective thing I found in trying to talk to them and calm them was to say, 'Let's say the Lord's Prayer,' and we would start, 'Our Father which art in heaven.' They had difficulty making it but they gradually began to form the words, and by the time we got to the end and they said the 'amen,' in so many cases they were completely calmed down. I know that a shell landing nearby might start the thing over again, but they were calmed down because they were doing something, they were saying something, their mind was completely off themselves and their situation and they were looking to God. Almost all of them knew the Lord's Prayer and we could use it."

I've quoted Reverend Craven's oral history fairly extensively because as the regimental chaplain, his experiences would have been similar to those of Father Griffin, whose accounts I've only been able to glean from newspaper articles and people who served with or knew him.

At one point, Craven said, he went for three days without sleep, and I'm sure Father Griffin and Mathew experienced similar deprivation; in fact, there was a stretch of 14 days during which Craven told his interviewer that he got no sleep.

From the Chaplain Corps history: "Once Craven was sent to an empty tent to rest and had hardly stretched out when another consignment of wounded arrived who were put in the same tent. Of course there was no opportunity then for sleep when the wounded needed help so desperately."

"That was at Yudam-ni, before we moved out of Hagaru-ri," Craven told the oral history interviewer. "I was at the regimental staff meeting on Sunday night before we were to move and our 7th Marine Regiment was to move up to the north toward Yudam-ni, around to the northwest. The colonel said to us as we closed the meeting, 'When we get up to Yudam-ni we will probably have communists sticking out of our ears, but that's where we are ordered to go so that's where we'll go.'

"The next morning we started the advance and the battalions of the 7th Marines went out. One battalion took a high point near Toktong Pass and Fox Company was left on the hill to protect us. We move on up to the Yudam-ni area where the 5th Marines were supposed to continue the attack to the north, but when we moved into position there, and just as soon as the 5th Marines started to move through us, the Chinese communists that had been building up, and building up, let loose with everything they had. I don't know how many divisions of communist troops there were but they came in from every side all over us and we started taking heavy casualties all night. I was with two corpsmen and we had no doctor in the area where I was and we were taking care of the wounded all night. ... The casualties continued that night, the next day, the next night, and then I moved to a combined air station where the 5th Marine Regiment and the 7th Marine Regiment (Mathew's) had their hospital and then a field hospital unit from the medical battalion of the division moved in and set up a lot of tents to take care of these casualties."

It was during this period, Craven said, that "we didn't sleep at all ... and in the early part of it before we had tents I sent men out and we got rice straw, and then in a big courtyard we put down this rice straw in this freezing weather way below zero. And then I got a big tarpaulin and we put these men down under it with their feet sticking in toward each other and their heads sticking out at the opposite end with the tarpaulin over and with the straw underneath to protect from the cold and treated and took care of these men the best we could until we finally got some tents. Of course we lost a lot of men."

Before leaving Yudam-ni, Craven conducted a funeral service for some 80 Marines. "The problems involved in attempting to bury bodies ... when the frozen ground was covered with ice and snow and the temperature about 20 below zero are beyond words to describe," he wrote.

From the 7th Regiment history: "On November 29, the forward elements of Marines, Royal Marine Commandos and U.S. Army troops who fought their way through from Koto-ri arrived with supplies. A rear element of the initial column had been turned back under fire. However, the bulk of the convoy had been overrun by the Chinese — 130 Marines, soldiers and Royal Marines captured.

"With the Chinese attacks repulsed, General [Oliver] Smith's Marines now repaired the airstrip at Hagaru and awaited the December 1 arrival of C-47s which would bring in supplies and evacuate the wounded. As supplies flowed into Hagaru, decimated Army units began to straggle into the Reservoir perimeter, and were placed under General Smith's operational control. About 450 soldiers were issued Marine equipment and formed into a provisional battalion.

"After four days on the defensive, the 5th and 7th Regiments took the initiative to break out from the vicinity of Yudam-ni and redeploy to Hagaru. The 1st Battalion of the 7th Regiment would seize the mountain pass and relieve Captain [William] Barber and the men of beleaguered Fox Company [whose story is told in "The Last Stand of Fox Company" by Bob Drury and Tom Clavin]. They set out at night on December 1, and linked up with Barber's company before noon on the Second.

Carrying their wounded, the remainder of the two regiments moved out shortly after daylight on December 2. As they withdrew under cover of air and artillery, swarms of Chinese followed, but rather than attacking, they were diverted to heaps of rubbish which the Marines had discarded.

"Close air support missions flown by the Air Force, Marine Corps and Navy provided a continual umbrella of bombs and bullets around the advancing column. And artillery fire from the perimeter at Hagaru provided an additional steel curtain to cut down attacking Chinese. With their single tank to blast roadblocks, the two regiments fought forward toward Lt. Col. Raymond Davis and his battalion at the pass. The units cleared the pass and moved inside the Hagaru perimeter on the morning of December 3. ...

"The fight from Hagaru to Koto-ri began on December 6, with elements of the 7th again on the road. Units would stage out, and General Smith made the decision to come out in a fighting withdrawal with every piece of salvageable equipment. The provisional Army battalion took the left flank, 2nd Battalion of the 7th [Mathew's] was on point, 1st on the right, and 3rd as rear guard. Tanks were up front to blast roadblocks. Overhead were tactical aircraft ready to deliver bombs and bullets in close support. There were an estimated 1,000 vehicles in the column. Only drivers, the wounded and a very few selected by unit commanders rode. Harassed by automatic weapons and mortar fire throughout the day, the column made slow progress while infantry skirmishes erupted.

"Chinese troops infiltrated and cut the column at night, and two blown bridges had to be repaired before they reached the Koto-ri perimeter during the morning of December 7." [It was during the night of December 6 that Mathew was killed.]

This is likely the ambulance in which Mathew was killed.

"One of the Finest Kids I Ever Knew"

In his book "Chosin: Heroic Ordeal of the Korean War," author Eric Hammel includes a dramatic account of Mathew's heroism.

"While the tiny companies of the 3rd Battalion, 7th, fought to control the Chinese buildup beside the road," Hammel wrote, "the convoy remained rooted to its position. Ranging the long column to help with the wounded, Father Connie Griffin, the 7th Regiment's Catholic chaplain, and his clerk, Sergeant Matt Caruso, climbed into the 3rd Battalion's cracker-box ambulance to administer the Last Rites of the Church to a young Mexican-American Marine who felt that his time had come. Griffin grasped the hand of the severely wounded youngster, stared into his dark eyes and spoke gently to him in his native Spanish, assuring him that all was well on the outside despite the sounds of gunfire.

"Among the wounded Marines looking on was Staff Sergeant John Audas, of Fox/7. He had spent most of the day lying wounded in a ditch across the road from Sangpyong-ni. He had nearly frozen to death before being discovered by fellow Marines at dusk and placed aboard the cracker-box ambulance and treated."

In Donald Knox's oral history of the Korean War, Father Griffin tells what happened next:

"The regimental train stopped outside of Koto-ri in the early hours of the morning (2 a.m., 7 December]. Sgt. Matt Caruso, my loyal clerk, and I climbed into a small ambulance to see if I could help anyone. The column was hit by enemy fire. Sergeant Caruso threw himself around me and screamed out, 'Look out, Father! Look out!' Those were his final words, as he was killed right there. More bullets smashed through the windshield. One struck me in the jaw and went out my back. I fell on top of Sergeant Caruso's body. Dr. Bob Wedemeyer yelled, 'Watch him.' I asked whether I was bleeding to death. Bob said, 'Don't let him exsanguinate!' (This meant, in Latin, 'run out of blood.') I told him I'd forgotten more Latin than he ever learned. A corpsman [Chief Pharmacist's Mate Peter Ciani] told me to shut up so they could go to work. Bob Wedemeyer then ordered Sergeant Caruso's body removed from the ambulance. I protested. He said to me, 'Padre, this ambulance is for the living, not the dead.'"

"During all my time in Korea I was in only one ferocious firefight," 90-year-old veteran George Howe, who fought in World War II and Korea, told author James Brady in "Why Marines Fight."

"On December 6, 7th Marine headquarters staff elements in their jeeps were headed out of Hagaru-ri in column near nightfall on the MSR. Mike Knott and I were walking behind a tank leading the way, Mike to my left. The tankers' hatch was open with a gunner at the ready with a .50-caliber machine gun. Following was the S-1 jeep, Pfc. Snedeker the driver, Captain Grove to his right in the passenger seat. The rear held two passengers, Second Lieutenant Balzer and Pfc. Rubio, both cowering behind the jeep windbreaker. The S-2 jeep followed with Captain France and his assistant First Lieutenant Clarence McGuinness, then the S-3 (ops) jeep, then HQ and Staff jeep with the First Sergeant, McCoy, and Staff Sergeant Cotton with his .30-caliber machine gun, a few clerks and Chaplain Cornelius 'Connie' Griffin with his driver and assistant, Sergeant Matthew Caputo." [Howe was 90 when Brady interviewed him, so he can be forgiven a senior moment.]

"'Suddenly,' Howe continued, 'from our left flank a fusillade of rifle and machine gun fire from the Chinese caught the headquarters staff in an ambush that came close to total disaster. Mike Knott immediately began returning fire with his carbine and in a moment he was wounded, knocked out of action. My carbine in hand, I heard Pfc. Richard Austin call to me, 'Sergeant, I'm hit.' He'd been hit in the back when he turned to reload his rifle, he told me. Laying my carbine down next to the tank I called out to Corporal Sandowsky to give me a hand. He replied, 'Sarge, we will never make it. Too much machine gun fire.'

"Howe wasn't buying it. 'F--- you,' he said. 'Get over here.'

"With me on one side and Sandowsky on the other we lifted and half dragged Austin to an ambulance forward of our position, maybe 50 yards ahead. The corporal and I returned to our ditch positions on the run, and resumed firing. Captain Grove attended to Mike Knott and neither Snedeker nor the other passenger were hit. Captain France and Lt. McGuinness were both killed trying to take cover in the roadside ditch. Later I saw their bodies where they fell. Chaplain Griffin's chin was shot away and Sergeant Caputo was killed.

"Cotton's .30-caliber gun and the tanker's .50-caliber machine gun fired in tandem during the ambush. Marine air arrived and dropped napalm on the Chinese. The firefight then came to an end as quickly as it started."

When I met Daniel Caruso, Mathew's son, for the first time since he was a toddler at the rededication of the Caruso Chapel in June of 2014, he said that someone told him — he didn't recall who or when — that the reason the ambulance came under fire was that another vehicle turned on its lights during blackout conditions.

In 2002, after seeing a letter I wrote to Leatherneck Magazine about Mathew, Michael J. Gregory sent me a copy of a story he'd sent to the Marine Corps History Archives.

"On or about Dec. 6, 7, 8, 1950, the night that Captain France, S-2, and Lt. McGuinness were killed in action," Gregory wrote, "the following incident took place. I am withholding the name of the driver of the jeep, who has since passed away, as I do not wish to embarrass his family.

"I call this incident, 'Where were you when the lights went on?'

"As the Regimental 7th column proceeded from Hagaru to Koto-ri, somewhere in the vicinity of Hell Fire Valley, leading the column was a USMC tank, followed by Colonel Litzenberg, Lt. Col. Dowsett, and Captain Zawaski, all in separate jeeps. Behind them was a jeep with a driver and a 300 SCR radio operator. Behind these vehicles were Captain France and Lt. McGuinness and their jeeps with trailers attached.

"The column was halted by a roadblock-ambush from our left flank. Automatic weapon fire raked the head of the column. Somehow, as the driver in the vehicle directly in front of our vehicles, attempted to exit his vehicle in haste, he turned on the lights of his vehicle. Whether he was attempting to shut off the engine, or what, we never did find out.

"As you can picture this, confusion on both sides emerged. We could see dead and wounded Chinese lying nearby. We assumed that they had been killed trying to bring up satchel charges to knock out the lead tank. When the lights went out — it seemed like eternity — Captain France told me to go forward to get more ammo from one of the trailers. At this point, as I went forward, all hell broke loose. I managed to pick up ammo and return to my position near Captain France's vehicle, only to find that both he and Lt. McGuinness had been wounded. I later learned that they had both been killed. Also wounded were Lt. Col. Dowsett and Captain Zawasky.

"Behind Captain France's jeep was an ambulance with a Red Cross on a white background. I am not certain, but I think this was the ambulance that was shot up badly and pictures of it have appeared in the Chosin Digest. In this vehicle was Father Griffin, administering last rites to wounded, and he was shot in the jaw. His assistant, Cpl. Matt Caruso, was killed during this incident.

"I cannot recall when we started to move out again. The next thing I recall was being south of Koto-ri waiting for the bridge to be rebuilt.

"You can see why I call my story 'Where were you when the lights went on?' Do you know if this is what you are looking for? I've never seen any reference to the incident, but recall rehashing it when we got to Masan."

Another account is in the Chaplain Corps history:

"The march south from Hagaru-ri to Koto-ri began on 6 December, only two days after the final elements of the Yudam-ni forces arrived at Hagaru. At 2230 of that day Chaplain Cornelius J. Griffin was seriously wounded when the ambulance in which he was riding came under severe machine gun fire. While en route to Koto-ri, Chaplain Griffin was giving the last rites of his church to a dying young Marine. With the chaplain was his assistant, Sgt. Mathew Caruso. On a narrow mountainous road leading into Koto-ri, the convoy ran into a roadblock. Although the ambulance was clearly marked with the Red Cross, such a symbol of mercy was not respected by the Communists. A machine gun bullet tore through the chaplain's lower jaw, causing a deep wound. Another bullet hit him in the right shoulder. Sergeant Caruso flung himself over his chaplain just in time to catch another bullet which took his life. In an interview published in the Monitor of 5 January 1951, Griffin said:

"'My clerk was killed as he lay alongside me. He was a 20-year-old [actually Mathew was 19] grenadier and rifleman assigned to cover me, one of the finest kids I ever knew, Sgt. Mathew Caruso of Rocky Hill, Conn. He never left me, saved me I don't know how many times and even covered me with his body. He died 20 minutes after I had given him Communion.'

"Chaplain Griffin was knocked unconscious by the terrific blow on the jaw. Word was quickly passed to Chaplain Craven, who was then about a mile away, that Chaplain Griffin had been wounded. When Griffin regained consciousness, he was aware that someone was bending over him trying to get him to say the Act of Contrition: *'O my God, I am heartily sorry for having offended thee ... and I detest all my sins ...'* As the wounded chaplain began to repeat the words of the Roman Catholic prayer, he realized that the one bending over him was none other than his friend, John Craven, a Baptist."

"It was nearing 2400 hours ... when 'Griff' got it," Reverend Craven wrote in "A Bullet for the Chaplain."

"We'd been under attack a way back, and 'Griff' was riding in an ambulance with four very badly wounded Marines. They all happened to be Catholics, and he was administering the last rites of the church. It was a desperate scene, as the ambulance lurched and swayed through the icy darkness; the staring, frightened eyes of the wounded men fixed on the face of the Padre; and he intoned *'Oh my God, I am heartily sorry for having offended thee ...'* and those who could, formed the words after him with pain-numbed lips.

"Suddenly a flare went up on the flanks; the red cross on the side of the ambulance offered a perfect target for some Red machine gunner; he blazed away — and the ambulance was riddled with bullets. Sergeant Mathew Caruso, who was helping Griff, anticipated the situation by a fraction of a second. Screaming 'DOWN!' he literally knocked the chaplain to the floor of the vehicle. In so doing, he saved Chaplain Griffin's life, at the sacrifice of his own; Caruso was dead when the firing stopped."

Although Craven referred to a flare illuminating the ambulance and Gregory wrote that it was the headlights of a jeep, Craven was some distance away when Mathew was killed.

"Chaplain Griffin took a bullet through the jaw; and sustained other wounds," Craven wrote. "It looked very much as if he would follow Caruso to the last muster before the throne of God. I was at the head of the column on the point when I got the word. I immediately made my way to the ambulance and swung aboard.

"'How you doing, Griff?' I asked, trying to keep my voice steady.

"'Not so good, John,' he managed to mumble, although half of his jaw hung loose, useless, and bloody.

"'I'd like to say a prayer, Griff.'

"'I'd appreciate it, John. ...'

"And so, as the ambulance bumped, rattled and floundered through the bitter Korean night, I, a Protestant chaplain, led Cornelius Griffin, a Catholic priest, in the 'Act of Contrition' of the Catholic church — for neither of us knew but what it would be his last prayer, and perhaps mine as well:

"'*I detest all my sins ... because they have offended Thee, my God, who art good and worthy of all my love. ...*'"

Many years later, in his oral history, Chaplain Craven would recall, "It was between Hagaru-ri and Koto-ri that the Chinese really laid into us. They had all kinds of ambushes and machine gun emplacements. I saw many more of those bluish-green tracer bullets that the communists used in their machine guns.

"It was during that time that several in our regimental headquarters were killed and wounded as we were moving forward. That's the night also that Chaplain Griffin ... was wounded. I got word that he had been wounded and I went back along the line to the ambulance. He was in an ambulance ministering to somebody when the ambulance was riddled with bullets and he was show up in there. And Sergeant Mathew Caruso, our chaplain's assistant, was killed in that ambulance. I got to visit with

Chaplain Griffin, just briefly. But his jaw was shot up and his shoulder was all shot up. The next morning at the aid station in Koto-ri we got to see him and spend some time with him.

"Then I went back down the line as we were moving down to Koto-ri and there were some incoming shells and machine gun bullets crossing the road. I heard a cry for a corpsman. I always carried a first-aid packet with me in combat. A corpsman had made it up for me and I always had it on my shoulder. So I rushed up to see who had been it. It was Colonel Dowsett, our regimental executive officer. I said, 'What's wrong?' He said, 'Chaplain, they got me in the foot.' His foot was all shot up, his ankle. So I got hold of him and put a battle dressing around that and got him into my jeep, and I went along with him as we continued on our way out.

"Before we left I picked up some little cans of peanuts and walnuts and things like that to take along for eating because you couldn't eat frozen food. The only way to eat the C-rations was if you might put a can underneath your arm under the parka in the morning when you started out hoping that it would be thawed out enough by evening to get a spoon into it. Most of us lost anywhere from 25 to 40 pounds during all this experience.

"I had given Colonel Dowsett some salted pecans which he was eating and pretty soon he wanted something to drink. Well, there was no water. All the water in the canteens was frozen. A few months later after we got out of Korea, I saw Colonel Dowsett at Annapolis. When I walked into the room to visit with him the first thing he said was, 'There's the guy that fed me salted peanuts and then didn't give me any water to drink afterward.'

"But that was a real difficult night between Hagaru-ri and Koto-ri (the night Mathew was killed). There were a lot of casualties. Our S-2 and Assistant S-2 of the regiment were killed. But the next morning we got into Koto-ri and into an aid station and I got to visit with Chaplain Griffin before he was evacuated by air. That's where the story started that I had said the last rites with him. This got played up during Brotherhood Week later on. Actually I just said a prayer with him in the aid station. He may have said that I said a prayer and then some people made the story from that.

"I had learned how to say the Act of Contrition or go over it with a dying Catholic fellow, but at that time I wasn't conscious of that. I was just having a prayer for him because of his being wounded."

Chaplain Connell J. Maguire

Nobility

Aware that Mathew's wife was soon to give birth, Father Griffin apparently tried to spare my brother from further combat. Mathew would have no part of it.

Robert McMillen, an Episcopal chaplain, was an instructor in the Navy's chaplain school after the Korean War. One of his students was a young Catholic priest, Connell J. Maguire, who would eventually serve as a chaplain in Vietnam.

In his memoir, "Foibles of Father Joe," Maguire recalled a lesson McMillen taught.

"Father McMillen taught us in Chaplain School in 1952," Maguire wrote. He was a buddy of Father Connie Griffin, and recounted for us this story about his friend.

"Chaplain Griffin was with the Marines in the Korean War. His clerk was a young enlisted Marine, probably of Corporal rank, named Caruso. Father Griffin learned that his battalion was going up to the front. He also knew that Caruso's wife was expecting back home. He had Caruso transferred from his staff so that Caruso would stay behind. Before the Battalion moved up, he ran into Caruso, who broke down and cried because, as he saw it, Father Griffin had fired him. So the chaplain relented and they moved up together.

"Chinese 'volunteers' had entered the fray and Marine casualties were heavy. They were pounded by artillery day and night. During a bombardment, Caruso touched the container of Holy Communion Griffin carried and said, 'He is with us.'

"They were not there long when one day Caruso saw an enemy set up a machine gun close by. 'Father look out!' he shouted. He shielded Father Griffin with his body. Immediately, he was stitched with machine gun holes across his body, dead on the spot. Father Griffin's jaw was shot off.

"I do not know whether the Caruso baby was a boy or a girl. He or she should be over 50 now, somewhere in New England if the grown child stayed near his parents' neighborhood. This I do know. People coddled and cuddled in luxurious living, selfishly indulging in sexual infidelity, claim the title of nobility. Their claim pales before the lineage of that Caruso child, offspring of a truly noble father."

The Telegram

"That Caruso child," my nephew Daniel, was born on Dec. 12, 1950, six days after Mathew was killed and a week before the telegram arrived.

The mood was festive in our household that month. There were two new arrivals in the family — Larry, Mike and Annabelle's second child; and Mathew — the holiday decorations were up, presents wrapped in newspaper comics were under the tree (who could afford wrapping paper?), and newspaper headlines were trumpeting the escape of the 1st Marine Division from the trap at the Chosin Reservoir. The newspaper accounts had been so dire we thought Mathew's entire division would be wiped out, but now we were sure he would be safe.

Mike and Annabelle went to the movies on the night of Dec. 19. It was their first night out since Larry was born. Peter was upstairs babysitting Carol and Larry, while I was in the living room watching Ralph and Billy playing on the floor. Then the doorbell rang.

The movie Mike and Annabelle went to see was "The Next Voice You Hear." It stars James Whitmore as "Joe Smith," a blue collar American working in an aircraft factory, and Nancy Davis — the future Nancy Reagan — as Joe's wife, Mary. Joe and Mary, hmmm. There's also a young son and a nagging mother-in-law who never misses an opportunity to remind Joe that Mary, who's expecting, lost both her mother and sister to complications from second pregnancies. Annabelle, Mike's wife, gave birth to her own second child two weeks before.

As the film opens, lettering on the screen announces "The First Day." In the evening Joe turns on the radio. Precisely at 8:30, following some music, an announcer says, "The next voice you hear ..." and presumably is about to introduce a singer. He's interrupted by the voice of God.

The week goes on with various crises in the family. Joe has a habit of backing his car out of the driveway without looking, at a high speed, and into the street, where a neighborhood cop who knows his routine is always waiting to pull him over and write him a ticket.

As "The Second Day" and the third and fourth and fifth pass, the radio audience around the world swells and swells until just about everybody on earth is glued to the radio at 8:30, never mind what time zone they're in or what language they speak. Mary wonders aloud whether it's some kind of hoax, like Orson Welles' broadcast of "The War of the Worlds" in 1938, which caused a nationwide panic because many people tuned in after the announcement at the beginning that the program was fictional. In "The Next Voice You Hear," a radio newscaster — played, without credit, by Chet Huntley according to the Internet Movie Database — points out that an Arab and a Jew, sharing a taxicab, both heard the voice of God, one of them in Hebrew and the other in Arabic.

On the seventh day, the voice goes silent. God is resting. Mary goes into labor, the second child is healthy, and all is well in the world. Even the neighborhood cop doesn't give Joe a ticket.

The movie is about the need for peace in the world following the devastation of World War II. Ironically, its premiere was on June 26, 1950, a day after the North Korean army crossed the 38th Parallel and the Korean War began.

When Mike and Annabelle came home that night, the next voice they heard wasn't mine. I was unable to speak. I didn't know what to say. I handed Mike the telegram. Mike turned ashen. Our father wasn't home yet from his carpenters union meeting, so Mike phoned Pat, who came over. When our father came home from a union meeting, Mike announced, "Mathew's dead." Dad didn't say a word, but the emotional pain was evident in his face. Mathew had pleaded with him to allow him to enlist at 17. Dad relented, and now was wracked with guilt.

That night, Mike and Pat closed down Shannon's, a local tavern. By the end of the evening the two World War II veterans were ready to re-up, although neither of them actually did.

Baby Will Get Medal Today For Father He Never Saw

DANIEL CARUSO

Deaths, Now At 29, Stir Civic Protests

Elizabeth Mayor Would Shift Field

All but Seven Victims Identified; Citizens to Hold Airport Meeting

Sailor Plays Pipe Organs, Must Face Music In Court

The Silver Star

I don't know whose idea it was to award Mathew's Silver Star to little Danny but it made the Hartford Courant, and today it likely would have gone viral.

"Daniel Caruso of 10 Birch Street, Rocky Hill, probably won't understand the ceremony in which he will take part at the Groton Submarine Base today," the article in the Courant on Jan. 24, 1951 begins. "He's only 14 months old.

"But he'll be given something which he will be able to keep always. It's the Silver Star medal which he will receive in the absence of his father whom he has never seen. ..."

"Today Daniel and his mother, Mrs. Robert Smith, who remarried recently, will visit the Submarine Base at Groton to receive the medal Sergeant Caruso earned with his life.

"Captain Charles O. Triebel, commanding officer of the Submarine Base, will pin the medal on Daniel during a base-wide personnel inspection."

A single column picture in the Courant the day before shows Danny, his eyes wide, beneath faint brows, with a full head of hair — he's a Caruso, after all — his lips open in a kind of triangle, wearing a shirt with a dog bounding across his chest, his little hands clasped together. The article, by Irving Kravsow, who would become a legendary managing editor of the Courant, describes little Daniel Caruso as 14 months old, although he was actually a couple of days shy of 13 months and two weeks.

As I remember it, the day was cold and overcast. I was about 16. Mathew's widow, Betty, was there without her new husband, Bob Smith, who she would say many years later — after he passed away — was always a little jealous of the time she shared with Mathew. My father was there. I don't recall if Mike was there, but I know if he was able to be he would have been.

Tom Tomlinson. *(Photo courtesy of the Robert F. Dorr collection.)*

'A Cold White Howling Beast'

In 2002 I wrote an article in "Leatherneck" magazine about my brother's sacrifice. Among the responses I received was a recollection of an encounter with Father Griffin perhaps only hours before he was wounded and Mathew was killed.

Tom Tomlinson was a World War II fighter pilot who joined the Marine Reserves in Michigan after the war. His unit was activated for Korea. He wrote a memoir titled "The Threadbare Buzzard: A Marine Fighter Pilot in WWII," published in 2004, about two years after he sent me the excerpts.

"John, it has taken me a long time but here are some excerpts from several items I wrote over many years," he wrote in an accompanying note. "My wife typed them up rather than having you try to read my handwriting [which, I might note, was not at all difficult to read]."

"Winter in Korea is described as a cold white howling beast," one of the excerpts begins. "It is not a dry cold. It's a wet, raw, devouring cold. Weapons froze, rations froze, human flesh froze. Mechanization broke down. Men crawled into their sleeping bags at night — never completely *in* because men surprised in their sleeping bags never live. C-rations had to be heated but only the outer parts thawed. A hard core of frozen food remained within and when devoured by a hungry man resulted in enteritis, or worse, diarrhea. Canteens froze and burst and men slaked their thirst by eating snow. Crackers were thawed in that single place of warmth — the human mouth. In this cold, blood also froze and plasma was useless. The cold did help wounded men by stopping the flow of blood, but to lie too long caused gangrene.

"120,000 Chinese came stealing in — hiding by day in caves, mine shafts and native huts, always moving and striking at night, their aim nothing less than annihilation of American troops. Night fighting was the way to go, primarily because the U.S. air and artillery support was not as effective as in the daylight hours. The Chinese completely surrounded the American, British and Turkish troops; however, General Smith, U.S. Marines, explained the campaign was going according to plan. He explained the military meaning of "retreat" was an orderly retirement to the rear forced upon you by the enemy. Here the enemy held the ground to the front *and* the rear. From this situation came the famous Marine philosophy of Korea: "Retreat hell, we're just attacking in another direction."

The excerpt from Tomlinson's book in which he describes his encounter with Father Griffin begins, "After returning from World War II I joined the Marine Corps Reserve in Detroit. At the outbreak of the Korean War our Reserve (17th Infantry) was called to active duty and sent to Korea, landing at Wonsan, North Korea, where we joined the 1st Marine Division on November 11, 1950."

"I joined a battery of the 11th Marines – an artillery unit," he continues. "We advanced to Koto-ri, Hagaru-ri and Udam-ni where the Chinese entered the rear and surrounded us. We fought back to Hagaru-ri where we reorganized and began our withdrawal to Koto-ri.

"My outfit began to withdraw the afternoon of December 6th. As we crossed a bridge just outside of Hagaru-ri, we received fire from the east hill to our left. My duty was manning a fifty caliber machine gun mounted on a 6 x 6 truck.

"Before we could fire, I was hit in my right arm and side. My right arm was broken. I was placed on a stretcher and put on an ambulance jeep. Shortly thereafter another person was put in the jeep where we spent the next 24 hours to travel the ten miles to Koto-ri.

"When we left the States I had carried two pints of Seagram's whiskey which I stored for any possible need. When we debarked at Wonsan I brought out one pint and split it with my buddies. Some of them wanted me to open the second bottle and I told them I was saving it for a future need. The night of December 6th was time for the second bottle. As my arm was broken I asked the other Marine, who I found out was a chaplain, to reach into my pocket and bring out the pint. He did and the corpsman, chaplain and I shared the pint. After finishing the pint the chaplain broke out his communion wine — which we shared."

In a ceremony at Pearl Harbor several months after he was wounded, Father Griffin was awarded the Silver Star for his heroism at Sudong-ni.

"They don't give a damn whom they shoot, do they, Chaplain?" Gen. Lemuel C. Shepherd said as he pinned the medal on Griffin.

As an aside, Tom Tomlinson, who sent me the excerpts from his then-unpublished book, told an anecdote about General Shepherd.

"As we progressed up the east side of the Chosin Reservoir with Col. Ray Murray's 5th Regiment," he wrote, "we passed a small village with a lumberyard. After setting up tents, I asked Captain Jordan to give me a truck and I would get flooring for the tents. While loading lumber at the lumberyard I saw some pine boxes – caskets – and thought they'd be great for use as outhouses. We loaded one on the truck. When we returned I told the captain of my plan and he told me where the property sergeant's tools were. I found a keyhole and soon had a three-seater with covers and a canvas windbreak. It was a real hit with all concerned. When we pulled back and proceeded up the west side of the Chosin Reservoir our outhouse came along strung by a cable on the battery's automotive wrecker.

"While 'fighting to the rear,' we somehow lost our outhouse.

"On December 4th we encountered a roadblock. I had mounted a .50-caliber on a Six by Six as we pulled out from Yudam-ni. The enemy firing coming from a valley on our right had all of us pinned down, including the infantry. Along with a loader I mounted a truck and began firing into the valley at our suspected enemy position. One was a large barn. Several Marines on the ground gave us the suspected position they thought the firing was coming from and we directed fire in those directions. All incoming fire ceased as the column moved out. ... Three days later out of Hagaru I was wounded. It took 24 hours to reach Koto-ri after dark on the 7th of December. I was driven out to a waiting torpedo bomber for evacuation. As I was being put aboard the plane, a jeep with correspondent Maggie Higgins and a couple of officers arrived. They were to take my place on the plane and they did. It snowed for the next three days and we had no air cover for evacuation of wounded. I was flown out on the third day on a C-47. Years later in talking with Eric Hammel, author of 'Chosin,' I learned the officer with Maggie Higgins was Marine Corps Commandant Lemuel Shepherd, Jr."

While Father Griffin was in the hospital, General Litzenberg, the 7th Regiment commander, paid him a visit.

"I knew at once what he would say," Griffin said in the oral history quoted by Donald Knox in "The Korean War: Pusan to Chosin."

"When I had discarded my Navy blue and gold and put on my Marine fatigues for the first time," Griffin continued, "I looked like the Sad Sack. Other Marines looked starched and fresh; I looked like a total and irreversible disaster and smelled like a barrel of mothballs. I was in Camp Lejeune in August, at the railroad loading dock and wearing my ill-fitting uniform, when I first had the privilege, not so regarded at that moment, however, of meeting my new commanding officer, the silver-haired fox, Homer Litzenberg, Colonel, United States Marine Corps. The great Litz said to me, not directly, you understand, but through the senior chaplain at whose side I stood, 'Jesus Christ, is this what I'm getting for a Catholic chaplain!' I spoke up: 'If the colonel knows, or can, in any way devise some way to ameliorate this messy situation, it will please the chaplain concerned. By your leave, Sir.' He replied, and this time he spoke directly to me, 'Get on that train, goddamn it! I'll make a Marine out of you even if it kills you.'

"Litz sat at the foot of my hospital bed. He grabbed my hand. 'Well, damn it to hell. I did exactly what I said I would, almost. I damn near killed you, but I sure as hell made a Marine out of you.' We laughed. But what a compliment."

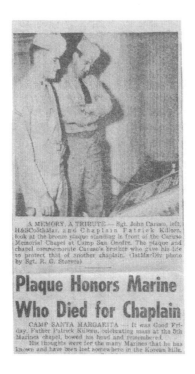

A MEMORY, A TRIBUTE — Sgt. John Caruso, left, H&SCo5thMar, and Chaplain Patrick Killeen, look at the bronze plaque standing in front of the Caruso Memorial Chapel at Camp San Onofre. The plaque and chapel commemorate Caruso's brother who gave his life to protect that of another chaplain. (1stMarDiv photo by Sgt. R. G. Stoeves)

Plaque Honors Marine Who Died for Chaplain

CAMP SANTA MARGARITA — It was Good Friday. Father Patrick Killeen, celebrating mass at the 5th Marines chapel, bowed his head and remembered.

His thoughts were for the many Marines that he has known and have been lost somewhere in the Korean hills.

That 38-Year Married Look

After the article appeared in Leatherneck Magazine I also got an email from Ken Young of Metairie, La. In the subject line it says: "Sgt. Mathew Caruso & Father Griffin, true story."

"At the risk of sounding somewhat presumptuous and having three friends who sit on the Federal Bench ... please, and I ask this respectfully, allow me to call you John. I'm a bit nervous, the reason for which will hopefully become apparent as I relate this story to you. That being said. ...

"Dear John: I regret not having the eloquence nor the vocabulary to do this simple, yet touching, story justice. Upon arriving home today I found my February issue of Leatherneck. Prior to having dinner with my wife, I did my usual once through quickly before I read each and every page in its entirety. Getting to page three was a breeze; however, when I saw the caption 'The Chaplain's Assistant at Chosin Reservoir,' I began to read. The first line of the second paragraph reads, 'He died saving the life of Navy Chap-,' John, before I turned the page, I said in my mind, 'Fr. Griffin.' So, turning the page, my heart skipped a beat when I saw the name Lieutenant Junior Grade Cornelius J. Griffin. I took the magazine downstairs and told my wife of 38 years that I had another story to tell her, but she had never heard this one before. Of course, I got that 38-year married look.

"Before beginning, I verified my graduation picture and certificate from the U.S. Naval Training Center, San Diego, which is dated 7-57. Easter Sunday normally falls in April. I do have the right time and place as I was in a sixteen-week yeoman course that eventually would lead me to becoming the Steno for then Maj. Gen. Edward Walter Snedeker, the Commanding General of the 1st Marine Division FMF [Fleet Marine Force], Camp Pendleton. General Snedeker replaced Gen. David M. Shoup who was moving to Washington to become our Commandant. A classmate of mine, Ron Swazy, went with General Shoup. I will gladly produce copies of both the picture, with date, and of the certificate, should you require them. Now, to the story. . .

"Cpl. Johnny Surugao and I became good friends. A Pole and a Hawaiian, which seems normal to me. Johnny was a 28-year-old Corporal and I a 19-year-old Private. One day while we were walking to the Chow Hall together, we saw brass coming towards us and naturally we stiffened up and gave our best salute, which was returned most casually yet with a warm smile. When we heard, 'How are you young men doing today?' as the brass stopped, we, too, stopped and politely answered, 'Fine, Sir, thank you.' It was then that I noticed the cross/crucifix on one collar and I believe an Oak Leaf on the other. Please remember, this was a long time ago. Certainly, the man was Father Griffin who engaged us in some small talk, where are you boys from, etc. Then, almost with apology, he said he didn't want to hold us up as he could see from the direction in which we were heading that we were heading for chow. We both hit attention again, this time smiling, and saluted. I must have had that puzzled look on my face that 19-year-olds are known to have. I'm sure that Fr. Griffin mentioned Koto-Ri; however, I could not swear to it, again, the passing of time. What I do more clearly recall is his saying that the young Marine must have spotted a reflection or movement of a sniper. He went on, 'As he threw himself at me, knocking me to the ground, he took the bullet which was no doubt meant for me. It went through him and left me with this (touching his scar).' Normal for a sniper to look for a collar with shiny brass on it, so no doubt Fr. Griffin was the target. At this point, his eyes were tearing, and I must freely admit so were Johnny's and mine. Johnny served in Korea.

"Well, we parted ways for the time being. Johnny and I retold the story to as many of the 20 to 30 Marines who were at NTC going to one school or another.

"Johnny and I are both Catholics and it was the week of Good Friday. In a way I'm kind of glad that I can't recall if it was Johnny's idea alone or mine as I'm not looking for false credit. I like to think that we worked it out together, and frankly, I think that is what happened. I seemed a bit more up on what goes on from 1500 on Good Friday until Easter Services. All Marines at the various schools were obliged to check their weapons with their home units prior to going to NTC so this part I know was from my mouth. I asked Johnny if he would come with me as I wanted to go 'next door' to the Marine Corps Recruit Depot. He agreed. We went, found the Chaplain, can't remember his name, and told him that we needed help in getting two M1s, no ammo, for the weekend and that we didn't have the time to go through channels. The good Father did the logical thing and asked us why we wanted them. We told him about Fr. Griffin, whom he knew, and that we had checked so that we wouldn't run into any flack. The gates at NTC were manned by the Navy. We got aboard OK and at the appropriate time, and shortly after Fr. Griffin left the chapel, we posted our first four hour watch. The guys were great and only about half were Catholic.

"Johnny and I drew, and this is a guess, the watch from 2200 until 0200. We left the front doors to the chapel wide open. Everyone, and John, I mean everyone took this watch very seriously. No grab ass or chit chat. Strict Parade Rest. Well, around 2300, with no one having been in the chapel for hours, we heard footsteps. As Fr. Griffin stood just far enough in front of us to be recognized, we pulled in the M1s and came to an Order Arms position. Not a single word was said. Fr. Griffin knelt on both knees facing the altar for about five minutes. He made the sign of the cross, got up, looked at both of us for what seemed an eternity, but was only a couple of minutes. He stepped towards Johnny, touched his shoulder and said, 'Thank you.' He then stepped towards me, touched my shoulder, and with choked voice said, 'Thank you.' I could see the tears freely flowing down his cheeks. He then quietly left.

"We maintained the watch, and it worked out so that Johnny and I were together for and during Easter Services. We held our posts until the service ended. Afterwards, Fr. Griffin invited us to join him in Easter Sunday breakfast. We had both taken the Eucharist, and frankly were hungry. Had to fast and abstain in those days before receiving Communion.

"Fr. Griffin thanked us and asked us to thank all the Marines who stood guard over his chapel. Johnny was designated to be our spokesman, though it wasn't much of a speech even though we both worked on it. John, Johnny told Fr. Griffin:

"'We were very happy to do this for you, Father. However, please know we also did it as much for the Marine you told us about and who could not be there to join us in person. We know he stood the watch with us in spirit.'

"This I remember as well as if it were yesterday.

"And, of course, I now know that the Marine we were referring to was your brother Sergeant Mathew Caruso.

"To Sgt. Caruso and to you, on behalf of Johnny, I say 'Semper Fi and God Bless both of you.'

"I don't believe this story is worthy of being put into your book. I do believe it is worthy of you knowing that this happened and that I am sure Fr. Griffin never, I repeat, never, forgot your brother.

"'I am not a writer and I sense that I may not have paid your brother nor Fr. Griffin justice in relating this story. If this is true, please accept my deepest apology. It has been many years and again, I lack the eloquence and vocabulary to do it the justice it deserves.

"Semper Fi,
'Kenneth A. Young
Former Corporal, USMC."

"You cannot exaggerate about the Marines. They are convinced, to the point of arrogance, that they are the most ferocious fighters on earth – and the amusing thing about it is that they are." **— Father Kevin Keaney, 1st Marine Division Chaplain, Korean War**

The Castoffs of Creation

Father Kevin J. Keaney, another Navy chaplain, was wounded at Koto-ri on Nov. 26, 1950. While it may not be as dramatic as "Retreat, hell!" his quote about the Marines has made its way into the lore of the Corps. When he was evacuated by air from Hagaru-ri, he was replaced by Chaplain Patrick A. Killeen, who was flown in by helicopter. In an odd twist of fate, Mathew worked for Chaplain Killeen before being assigned to Father Griffin.

I met Father Killeen at Camp Pendleton after the war. The local newspaper ran an article with a photo of him and me outside the Caruso Chapel. The headline says "Plaque Honors Marine Who Died for Chaplain."

The article, datelined Camp Santa Margarita, begins: "It was Good Friday. Father Patrick Killeen, celebrating Mass at the 5th Marines Chapel, bowed his head and remembered.

"His thoughts were for the many Marines that he has known and have been lost somewhere in the Korean hills. Straightening, he prepared to begin the Offertory when he saw a face and shuddered.

"A week passed before the padre was able to meet and identify the seemingly resurrected face that had jolted his memory back through the years. It belonged to Sgt. John Caruso, H&S [Headquarters and Service] Company, 5th Marines, but the memory was of another Sgt. Caruso — John's brother Mathew.

"Father Killeen, new to the Chaplain Corps, first met Mathew Caruso at Camp Lejeune where the Marine sergeant served as his assistant. An unexpected transfer took the Father to California and then overseas to Korea. But it wasn't long before their paths were to cross again. Caruso, now assisting Father Cornelius Griffin, was sent to Korea, also. The trio met briefly at Hagaru-ri before Caruso's outfit pushed on.

"When next Father Killeen saw the chaplain and his assistant, it was to perform last rites for them. Sgt. Caruso was dead. Father Griffin was critically injured and expected to die shortly, but he recovered and told Father Killeen an account of bravery that still burns in his memory.

"'The move was on; back from the Chosin Reservoir came the war weary and weather beaten Marines. At Koto-ri, Father Griffin moved among the men, administering first aid where necessary and performing last rites for Leathernecks beyond help. Night fell and Father Griffin set up a mercy station within a displaced ambulance. Sgt. Caruso continued to circulate among the men, pausing only to serve the needs of the wounded.

"'The Father called to his assistant, asking him to come out of the cold for a moment and help him in the ambulance. As Caruso stepped inside, a burp gun rattled and sprayed the vehicle.

"'Screaming 'Father — get down!' Caruso threw himself between the priest and flying rounds. He died instantly, his body riddled.'

"For his supreme sacrifice and heroism, Sgt. Mathew Caruso was nominated for the nation's highest award, and posthumously received the Silver Star.

"Father Griffin returned to the States and was not to forget the Marine who had laid down his life for him. Stationed at Camp Pendleton's Camp San Onofre, the Father initiated an idea to perpetuate Caruso's deed and memory.

"Caruso Memorial Chapel at Camp San Onofre now stands in lasting tribute. In front of the chapel, a bronze plaque bears a familiar but pertinent quote:

"'Greater love than this hath no man, that a man lay down his life for his friend.'"

If Gen. Oliver Smith's "Retreat, Hell! We're advancing in a different direction," is the most famous quote to be associated with the Chosin campaign, the chaplain Father Killeen replaced in Korea is credited with another of the most famous quotes in the history of the Corps.

"You cannot exaggerate about the Marines," Father Keaney wrote after being wounded. "They are convinced, to the point of arrogance, that they are the most ferocious fighters on earth — and the amusing thing about it is that they are. You should see the group about me as I write — dirty, beaded, their clothing food-spattered and filthy — they look like the castoffs of creation. Yet they have a sense of loyalty, generosity, even piety greater than any men I have ever known. These rugged men have the simple piety of children. You can't help loving them, in spite of their language and their loose sense of private property. Don't ever feel sorry for a priest in the Marines. The last eight weeks have been the happiest and most contented in my life."

Joe DiMaggio and Lefty O'Doul

"VA mental health clinicians counseling war veterans say that the veteran often agrees to a feeling as though there is a cemetery within their soul."

— Stanley Modrak, in "A Hostage of the Mind"

Here's to You, Joe DiMaggio

In 1985 Stanley Modrak, the Marine over whom Father Griffin recited the last rites at Sudong-ni, learned of a reunion of the "Chosin Few," as veterans of the battle came to be known. On the second night of the reunion, he wrote in his memoir, "just prior to dinner I was introduced to a black-garbed, somber Chaplain. Not just *any* Chaplain, but Father Cornelius 'Connie' Griffin ... who had performed the last rites over me that dark and traumatic night so long ago. What an unexpected and thrilling meeting! We shook hands as I thanked him for his care and words that dark, traumatic night on the Sudong battlefield.

Father Griffin didn't say much and his deep-set eyes seemed to have a haunted look about them. I'm sure that the reunion had brought back many, many disturbing memories of North Korea and of his bleak experiences at the Chosin during the breakout.

"Father Griffin's facial features were somewhat emaciated and scarred with his formerly dark hair now graying. I learned later that his cheek and jaw were hit with rounds from Chinese machine guns and that his assistant was killed instantly. Though Chaplain Griffin and his assistant were aiding and comforting wounded Marines in a panel truck with large Red Cross symbols on both sides, it didn't matter to the Chinese gunners."

At the reunion, Modrak learned of the death of one of his team members and the severe wounding of another, neither of whose names he could remember.

"VA mental health clinicians counseling war veterans say that the veteran often agrees to a feeling as though there is a cemetery within their soul," he wrote. "They feel an overweening responsibility that they must honor and not forget their lost dead comrades. They can be tortured with shame or remorse if they forget a name, a face, an event that involves a comrade. This I can agree with as I had previously mentioned how forgetting the names of our team's severely wounded officer and the death of our team sergeant had evoked shame and remorse even to this day — many years later."

Six years after that reunion, another event was to bring Modrak a bit of closure.

Google "Joe DiMaggio and Hamhung" and you'll find a video on YouTube of DiMaggio visiting wounded Marines at Hamhung, North Korea, on November 12, 1950. He signs a baseball for one Marine. Lefty O'Doul, who accompanied DiMaggio, signs a baseball for another.

One of the Marines for whom DiMaggio autographed a baseball was Stanley Modrak, the Marine for whom Father Griffin had recited the last rites just a few days before.

"Sometime in December" Modrak wrote in his memoir (although according to the video, he's a little off on the month), our hospital room had an unexpected and unusual pair of visitors. One afternoon two tall figures clad in heavy parkas and fur caps appeared. The famous baseball icon and New York Yankee superstar, Joe DiMaggio, known as the 'Yankee Clipper,' was at my bedside. Wow! Right in the middle of a 'Hot

War'; I couldn't believe my eyes. As a rabid baseball fan and admirer of DiMaggio, his appearance was a Korean War memory I'd never forget. Joe was accompanied by 'Lefty' O'Doul, a baseball star in his own right and DiMaggio's friend and mentor going back to their San Francisco ball-playing days. Right here in North Korea and not too far from the action, Joe and 'Lefty' were braving the bone-chilling North Korea winter to visit and cheer up American hospitalized military. This unselfish act greatly enhanced my admiration for Joe. I also knew that in the pantheon of Yankee greats only the 'Babe' ranked higher.

"Asking how I felt, Joe handed me an authentic American League baseball autographed with his distinctive signature. Turning the ball over it read: 'To Stanley, best wishes — Joe DiMaggio.'

"Overwhelmed, all I could do was murmur 'Gee. Thanks Joe.' After DiMaggio and O'Doul left, still not ambulatory, I gave the ball to our room corpsman to mail home for me to Pittsburgh. Big mistake! When I returned home some months later I learned that my wonderful trophy never arrived: What a disappointment! It probably was either stolen or lost in the wartime mail. As rabid baseball fans would understand, the loss bothered me for years after Korea. Having this uplifting experience in the midst of war and then the loss, I'm sure you can understand my feelings."

"Forward to a sultry L.A. summer in 1991," Modrak writes later in his memoir. "The loss of the DiMaggio baseball still caused regrets over the years as the 'Clipper' would be in the news from time to time. His marriage to Marilyn Monroe was prominent, then his devotion to her memory as he placed flowers on her grave site every year on their anniversary.

"The much-valued baseball and its loss seemed to be another layer of depression added to the other somber and regretful Korean War memories. My wife, Roulti, knew the story of the 'lost trophy,' as I had referred to it over the years and she realized how much it troubled me.

"Near my birthday in July of 1991 I checked the mail, finding a few letters, a bill and a small, square box. Curious, I turned it over to find that it bore the return address of the Oakland Athletics Baseball Club. Wondering what it could be, I eagerly opened the intriguing package. It held an authentic American League baseball. Turning the ball over, autographed words read: 'To Stanley, a replacement — Best Wishes, Joe DiMaggio.' Wow! After 41 years — what a birthday present!

"Happily showing the prized ball to my wife, she smiled with a knowing grin, admitting that it was her doing. A week earlier I had mentioned to her that DiMaggio was to be honored at an A's game celebrating his 56-game hitting streak in 1941. Remembering the lost-ball story, she had phoned the Oakland A's offices and spoke to general manager Sandy Alderson. As it turned out, Alderson was also a former Marine. So that coincidence along with my wife's feminine persuasion struck a responsive chord with Alderson — and DiMaggio."

Bulkeley High School Principal Gayle Allen-Greene presents Mathew's posthumous diploma, along with a cap and gown, to John Caruso in May of 2014.

The Radio Man

I graduated from Bulkeley High School in Hartford when I was 17 and wanted to go into the service right away to avenge Mathew's death, but my father wouldn't let me, so I had to wait until I turned 18.

There was another reason, though, that I wanted to enlist: I didn't have any illusions about going to college. In high school I took industrial arts courses. I took mechanical drawing and architectural drawing, wood shop, metal shop, everything connected with construction. I thought I'd follow in my father's footsteps and be a builder, and hopefully someday I'd be an engineer.

I didn't go into the Marines right away. I wanted to enlist in the Air Force. I loved flying. I used to build and fly model airplanes. A buddy of mine and I took some lessons, we weren't qualified to solo, but I loved airplanes and everything about them.

I wanted to be a pilot, but the Air Force told me I couldn't fly because I had a heart murmur. So I joined a group of my friends and we went to the post office, where they had the recruiting station, and we said we wanted to be paratroopers. Then they showed us a film about World War II, with men jumping out of planes and being shot in their parachutes on the way down. I said the heck with this, I want to be able to shoot back

I was thinking about going down to the Army recruiters because I didn't think I would survive the Marine Corps, being the scrawny kid that I was. But I ran into a Marine recruiter who actually was at the Chosin Reservoir with Mathew, and he talked me into enlisting.

I went for my physical in Springfield, Mass. They make you do some calisthenics to get your heart pumping, but they came over to me, I guess I was kind of pale, and they said "You'd better go lie down." So I did. A half-hour later I was practically asleep when the doctor came over and said, "You're OK." So they took me.

The next thing I know, I went to Parris Island for basic training, and I really grew to love the service. I liked the discipline. With my father out of the house and eight boys, there wasn't a lot of discipline at home. Now they told me when to get up, when to go to bed, and I learned how to keep everything clean, and to make sure you use your time quickly.

Basic training was 12 weeks, and our platoon was an honor platoon, so when we graduated we led the review of the troops.

We got a couple of weeks of leave after basic training. Some of the men in my platoon were from the South but most of us were going north, and there were a lot of platoons that graduated at the same time, so the train was packed.

But before we got on the train, we had to take a bus. It was a civilian bus, not a military bus. And we had two African-Americans in my platoon. Great guys. We got on the bus and the bus driver tells the African-Americans they have to sit in the back of the bus.

We'd just spent twelve weeks with these fellows and we didn't give a second thought about the color of their skin. Even the Southern boys accepted them and we had no problems. So two of the bigger guys in the platoon grab the bus driver and throw him off the bus, and one of them takes over the driving.

Meanwhile, the MPs are waiting for us. They surround the bus, and some of them get on the bus. Of course the guy driving the bus got the heck off the driver's seat and went to the middle of the bus. And one of the MPs says, "Which one of you threw the driver off this bus and drove the bus hee?"

And we all raised our hands. I think the MPs were somewhat sympathetic to us because they didn't press us further.

After my leave I went back to Parris Island and they asked me what I wanted to do. The Korean War was still on, and I said, "I want to get a rifle and go over and kill those bastards that killed my brother."

They must have thought I was fairly intelligent because they said, "We have a lot of guys that are riflemen but we need people in communications. You're going to be a radio man."

That sounded pretty good. I said, "What do I do as a radio man?"

"You carry a radio."

"What do you mean, I carry the radio?"

"You carry it on your back. And you're assigned to the second lieutenant."

Now I'm getting suspicious. "What does the lieutenant do?"

"He's in charge of deploying the platoon and making sure everybody's ready and well-trained, and he tells the sergeants where to take their squads." I was just a Pfc.

I said, "What kind of a platoon is it?"

"It's an infantry platoon."

I didn't think too much of it. I figured I'm carrying the radio, I'm staying next to the second lieutenant.

Then we went to Camp Pendleton for combat training. That was four weeks. They didn't work on your mind like they did in boot camp. They wanted you physically fit, and the training was tough. What we would call mountains in Connecticut, they called hills, and you had to go up them with full gear. They were a little less hard on you mentally than they were in boot camp. And out of 72 in my platoon who graduated from basic training, only 17 were assigned to go overseas.

When I got to Korea, I realized very quickly that carrying the radio and being next to the second lieutenant was not the safest place to be. The enemy tries to take out the second lieutenant. Then they take out the communications, and they take out the automatic weapons, to cut down on the firepower. So the first time we got into a firefight I was practically eating the dirt, and the bullets were flying overhead, and of course my antenna is sticking up. I thought to myself, "I thought was too damn smart to be in the infantry, and now I'm one of the first three that they try and get rid of."

I was in Korea for four and a half months at the end of the war. Then I was sent to Okinawa as a radio operator during a series of war games, but the largest part of my time in the Marines was spent in Japan as a communications chief.

As for Bulkeley High School, a lot has changed in the decades since most of the Caruso siblings attended classes there. The school is in a new building, and has grown so large that it has two principals, one for the upper classes and one for the lower. At an assembly in May of 2014 in which Mathew was posthumously awarded a diploma, along with a cap and gown, the keynote speaker was a recent graduate who spent time in Hollywood with some hip hop and rap stars I'd never heard of, yet he was clearly a role model and got a rousing reception from the hundreds of students in the audience.

After the assembly there was a reception in Bulkeley's History Center.

Prominent in the center is a portrait of Morgan Gardner Bulkeley, the school's namesake.

A display about Mathew was added for the ceremony, but there's an interesting juxtaposition between the creation of the history center a year earlier and Chaplain Evan Adams' constant retelling of Mathew's story to young Marines at Camp Pendleton.

"These days, 'students don't know who he is,'" Lou Frasca, the dean of students and a 1988 Bulkeley graduate, said in an article in the Hartford Courant.

Bulkeley was the mayor of Hartford, the governor of Connecticut, a United States senator, and the president of the Aetna Insurance Company, one of Hartford's major employers. He also is in the Baseball Hall of Fame for his role as the first president of the National League when it was formed in 1876, according to the article. He died in 1922.

On a wall in the back of the history center is a bronze plaque with the names of all of the Bulkeley students who died in World War II. A brief visit to the Internet revealed some surprising details about the names on the plaque.

According to a 2002 article in the Courant, a Vietnam veteran named Ken Roach was driving home from Hartford to Windsor, Connecticut, when he noticed a sign for what he remembered as the Whitehead Highway, "a short stretch of expressway" running from the Pulaski Circle to Interstate 91.

Roach learned that the stretch of road was named after Ulmont I. Whitehead Jr., one of the names near the bottom of the second row of names on the plaque in the Bulkeley History Center, which is arranged in alphabetical order.

"I discovered that Whitehead was killed in Pearl Harbor," Roach told Courant reporter Melissa Pionzio in that 2002 article. Which led him to think, "Why did we name a highway after this guy and he seems to have been forgotten?"

Roach learned that Whitehead graduated from Bulkeley in 1933 and enlisted in the Navy. He was assigned to the USS Mississippi "and was sent to Havana during an uprising there," according to the article.

That uprising was the so-called "Sergeants' Revolt," which was led by Fulgencio Batista. The revolt forced Cuba's then-dictator, General Gerardo Machado, to flee Cuba, according to an article titled "U.S. Warships in Cuban Waters," by John Young of the Universal Ship Cancellation Society, a group of collectors of postal service first-day covers.

"President Roosevelt sent thirty warships to protect our interests in Cuba," Young wrote. One of those ships was the battleship USS Mississippi.

Whitehead "won an appointment to Annapolis in 1934 and starred on Navy football teams in 1938 and 1939," Roach told the Courant. He "went on active duty after commencement and served on the USS Arizona at Pearl Harbor. He was on board the ship on December 7, 1941 ... and, at 26, he became the first Hartford resident to die in World War II. His body, along with those of 1,101 fellow servicemen, remains entombed on the ship in the waters of Hawaii."

The Chapel

"Dear Mike," the letter from Father Griffin, dated 30 March, 1953, begins. "Just a note to answer your grand weather. So very glad you have found a home to your liking.

"Yes, I have the wonderful picture you sent to me. I wrote an answer to you but perhaps you did not get it. I do not understand why it failed to arrive. I had it framed in a beautiful and expensive frame which such a rfine piece of art and so beautiful a memory deserves.

"As things stand now it looks like the new chapel in my camp will be named for Matt. I hope this goes through. It shall be called 'The Caruso Memorial Chapel.' The chapel cost around $50,000. I believe it is a permanent building, even though it's made out of aluminum.

"My live and blessing to you all and the Most Blessed of Easter joy.

"Devotedly in Christ, Father G."

[The caricature of Mathew, drawn by my brother Mike, hangs in the Caruso Memorial Chapel today and is engraved on the plaque at the chapel's entrance.]

An article in the Pendleton Scout of January 9, 1953, shows Father Griffin standing before the altar of the Caruso Chapel. Beneath the picture is the headline "Heroic Sergeant Who Sacrificed His Life In Korea Leaves Memorium."

"Lieutenant Cornelius J. Griffin, veteran of the Seventh Marines' historic withdrawal from the Chosin Reservoir," the article begins, "recently assumed duties as Catholic Chaplain for Tent Camp 2's Second Infantry Training Regiment."Behind the story of Lieutenant Griffin's new assignment is the story of a courageous Marine sergeant. A Marine who gave his life that Father Griffin might continue to administer to the spiritual needs of his fellow men.

"This Marine's name was Mathew Caruso. His story begins in the very chapel where Father Griffin now holds daily Mass.

"With the outbreak of hostilities in Korea, Camp San Onofre, known best by trainees as Tent Camp 2, was reactivated. Marines trained there, as they will do for combat with the First Marine Division in Korea.

"Realizing the need for a Catholic chapel, Sergeant Caruso, himself a trainee, collected old packing crates and constructed a makeshift chapel within a quonset hut.

"After completion of training at Camp Pendleton, Caruso was assigned to the Seventh Marine Regiment in Korea, where he served as assistant to Father Griffin. ...

"Father Griffin now holds daily Mass for men of the Second Infantry Training Regiment in the chapel begun by Sergeant Caruso.

"The chapel stands as a monument to a man who gave his life for God and Country; a man who died defending the principles in which he believed.

"Father Griffin's statement expresses his feelings: 'Caruso, and many like him, had enough love in their hearts to die so that we might live. We would do well to live for the principles for which they died.'"

FOUR

Chaplain, Saved By Marine, To Say His Funeral Mass

On Dec. 6, 1950, a Hartford Marine died a hero's death in Korea, shielding the body of a Catholic chaplain. Monday that chaplain, the Rev. Cornelius J. Griffin, will say the funeral mass in St. Augustine's Church for the man who saved his life.

Sgt. Matthew Caruso was 20 years old when he was killed by enemy machine gun fire while trying to save the Navy chaplain during the gallant retreat of the First Marine Division from the Chosin Reservoir.

Body on Way

Wednesday a telegram from the Marine Corps notified Caruso's family that Sgt. Caruso's body was enroute to Hartford. Marine Cpl. John R. Caruso, the dead sergeant's younger brother, is escorting the body.

The telegram stated that Sgt. Caruso's body would arrive in Hartford Saturday at 3:11 p.m. Naval officials were notified and Lt. Griffin was authorized to come to Hartford to officiate at the funeral Monday.

In 1952, Sgt. Caruso's 14-month-old son Daniel, who never saw his father, was given his father's posthumously awarded Silver Star at ceremonies at the Groton Sub Base. A year later a non-denominational chapel at Camp Pendleton, Calif., was dedicated in Sgt. Caruso's name.

SGT. MATTHEW CARUSO

The sergeant attended Bulkeley High School for three years before he enlisted in the Marines. He married the former Elizabeth Russell, who has since remarried, early in 1950 and left for Korea in August, 1950.

He was the son of Michael J. Caruso Sr. of Hartford and the late Harriet Parnell Caruso.

Besides his father, son and brother, he leaves six other brothers, Michael J. Caruso Jr. of East Hartford, George W. Caruso of Torrington, and Patrick D., Ralph F., Peter P. and William E. Caruso, all of Hartford; and two sisters, Mrs. Ralph Brooks of East Hartford, and Mrs. Theresa Houle of White Plains, N.Y.

The Thomas F. Farley Funeral Home, 96 Webster St., is in charge of funeral arrangements which are incomplete. Burial will be in Mt. St. Benedict Cemetery.

Full military honors will be accorded at the funeral.

Deaths

[illegible]

Obituary

Mrs. Grace O. Demers

Mrs. Grace Ouimette Demers, formerly of Kerr St., widow of George N. Demers, died at St.

Mathew's Funeral

It was raining when I arrived in San Francisco to meet the ship carrying Mathew's remains. He was buried in a mass grave at Koto-ri among some 60 fallen Marines and British commandos. One of his dogtags was placed on his tongue — this, I was told, is why the dogtags are grooved — to ensure he could be identified.

As I stood on the platform while the casket was being transferred to the freight car at the Union Street station, it was hard to be anonymous or to hide my emotions. My Class A uniform with my Korea ribbons and the black armband all but announced the nature of my mission.

Most of the people on the train were traveling either to Chicago or all the way across country. I was the only passenger in uniform and wearing a black armband, and I had on my United Natios and Korean Service medals.

The first time I went to the club car to have a meal, the elderly woman who asked me about the armband on the platform — elderly, heck, she was probably ten years younger than I am now — was sitting at a table with her husband, and she motioned for me to join them. When the bill came, they insisted on picking up the tab.

After that, I couldn't buy a meal, I couldn't buy a drink, not even a soda. People would ask me to sit down with them, and I'd tell them about Mathew. Women would start to cry. And the people were just wonderful.

But it was a bittersweet experience. It was a beautiful trip, but it was for a purpose that was sad.

When the train pulled into Hartford's Union Station, my father was there, along with Betty, who had remarried; her mother, and several of my brothers. My father was off standing by himself. He was a short man, only 5-foot-1. I began to walk towards him, and Mrs. Russell, Betty's mother, came across and grabbed me and hugged me and started talking, and I couldn't get away. I wanted to see my father because he was all by himself. Eventually I broke free and went to him. His face was pale and he had a sadness in his eyes that I'd only seen once before, the night Mike handed him the telegram.

My father thought they should open the casket to make sure it was Mathew, but both my older brother and I said, "Dad, he's been buried for five years. He's been in the ground."

"But how do we know it's Mathew?"

"Dad, they had graves registration, they had forensic evidence, they don't just willy nilly say 'This is your son' and throw some bones in a casket." I said, "They positively identified him. They even had his dogtag."

The remains were taken from the train station to the Farley Funeral Home on Webster Street in the South End of Hartford. When the telegram came five years earlier, all we could have was a memorial service. There was no body to bury.

This time, the funeral, like the presenting of the Silver Star to Mathew's toddler son, made national headlines, at least in the Catholic press.

"A postscript to one of the most moving stories of the Korean War was written here," an article sent out by the NCWC (National Catholic Welfare Council) News Service, datelined Hartford, said, "as a Navy chaplain crossed the continent to offer the Funeral Mass for the Marine who died saving the chaplain's life in the bloody retreat from the Chosin Reservoir nearly five years ago.

"Father (Lt.) Cornelius J. Griffin sang the Mass in St. Augustine's Church here for Marine Sgt. Mathew Caruso, whose body arrived back in his boyhood city from Korea. Father Griffin received special permission to leave his post as chaplain on the USS Sperry on the West Coast so that he could come here and offer the Mass."

The funeral was quite an event. In addition to Father Griffin, a monsignor and two other priests also celebrated the funeral Mass. All of us Caruso kids from the time my family moved to Hartford from Tarrytown, N.Y., went to St. Augustine School, and the Caruso name was pretty well known in the South End of Hartford.. The school was let out early and many of the pupils came to the funeral. Mike and Annabelle both worked for the state police, so the state police escorted the funeral procession. They had police cars blocking the intersections of the road after we left the church and went to Mount St. Benedict Cemetery in Bloomfield, right on the Hartford-Bloomfield border. My father and mother, my father's mother and father, and his first wife, who died at age 26, and now Mathew, are all buried there.

The Marines had a rifle team at the funeral, there was a riderless horse, and the buglers played triple Taps. It was just the most eerie feeling, the triple Taps, because it's like an echo. And when the Marines took the flag off the coffin because they were going to lower the coffin into the grave, they gave the flag to my father. I was a little surprised because Betty was there, but she had remarried, and I think the Marines felt it better belonged to my father.

Another press release, although I'm not sure of its origin, gives further details of the funeral:

"Sgt. Mathew R. Caruso's body arrived at the Hartford railroad station at 3:11 p,n,m" the release begins, "escorted by Cpl. John R. Caruso, his brother. He was accorded full military honors and is buried in lot 727-8, Section L, Mt. St. Benedict Cemetery in Bloomfield, CT.

"Rev. Cornelius J. Griffin was the celebrant at St. Augustine, whose school Matt graduated and whose boy's brigade Matt served as an officer before his enlistment.

Rev. John F. Cotter was the deacon and Rev. Thomas H. Dwyer was sub-deacon. Rt. Rev. Msgr. Thomas P. Mulcahy, Rt. Rev. Msgr. Leonard T. Wood and Rev. Leonard P. White were present in the sanctuary. Goode and White were former Navy chaplains.

Mrs. Elvia C. Strom was soloist. Bearers were all USMC members.

"Griffin, Dwyer, Good and White conducted committal services at the cemetery. A Marine firing squad and a Marine bugler performed at burial services. The American flag was folded and resented to Father Griffin who in turn presented it to Matt's father, Michael J. Caruso. Father Griffin at the time served aboard the USS Sperry, a destroyer stationed at San Diego.

"On Thursday, January 4, 1952, at Groton Submarine Base, 14-month-old Daniel Caruso and Michael J. Caruso were presented Silver Stars.

"On Wednesday, July 25, 1953, the non-sectarian chapel at Tent City Camp II (Camp San Onofre), Camp Pendleton, CA, was named the Caruso Memorial Chapel, the only one of its kind named for an enlisted man killed in action.

"Father Griffin was born in Indianapolis, IN. He had a brother, Charles (Chuck), who was a Navy veteran. When Chuck was buried, the soloist played 'Give My Regards to Broadway' at his exit from the church.

"Frather Griffin became a priest after graduating from Pontifical College Josephinum in Worthington, OH.

"Tommy Cook played Matt in 'Marines in Review,' an ABC coast-to-coast radio broadcast in the early '50s."

The Caruso Chapel was dedicated in 1953. About a dozen years ago I was in touch with the chaplain there, and that's when I started thinking about writing Mathew's story, because the chaplain gave me the impression that the base was going to close it down. I was worried about the picture Mike drew that's hanging in the chapel, and I feared that without the chapel Mathew would become a forgotten story of the forgotten war.

Then, in 2009, "Taking Chance," with Kevin Bacon, was shown on HBO. A reviewer on the International Movie Data Base says the film is "based on perhaps the single most moving artifact to come out of the Second Gulf War." Bacon plays Lt. Col. Mike Strobl, who accompanies the body of a 20-year-old Lance Corporal Chance Phelps, who was killed in the war across the country by plane. "There's no overstating the power and beauty of what he encountered: one instance after another of not just military personnel but airline employees, passengers and bystanders doing honor — mostly wordlessly — to Chance's coffin and his escort as they passed by." Although the wars and the mode of transportation were different, seeing the movie, I relived my trip across country with Mathew's body.

I again contacted the lead chaplain and expressed my concerns. "Tear it down?" he said. "Are you kidding? There's no way they're going to tear it down. We've got two chaplains out here, your brother's picture is in the foyer where it's been for 62 years. We service the entire School of Infantry, and we have thousands of young men going through advanced training. And it's a non-denominational chapel, anybody can go there, and a lot of guys do! " (Probably, I thought, to doze off instead of working on a detail, that's what we did in boot camp.) Then I found a YouTube video of members of the Church of Latter Day Saints painting and landscaping the chapel, where the chaplain told me the Mormons hold services twice a week.

John Caruso

Becoming a Lawyer

If it weren't for Mathew, the Corps, and my brother Mike, I probably would have followed my father into construction, and never would have become a lawyer, and later a judge.

Just before I got out of the service, Mike said, "I think you should go to college."

I said, "I don't have any money."

He said, "You're going to get a GI Bill. It's not as generous as the one we had after World War II, but it will be something."

Then I said, "I can't get into college. I have to take the college aptitude test." I was home on leave. It was the last leave before I got discharged. I had met my first wife and we were dating. We were at her house, with her parents, it was snowing heavily, and I had to take the test the next day at the old Hartford High School. I walked. Even the snowplows were stuck. I walked all the way from Wethersfield to my house, and I just about got there and I had to walk to Hartford High School, which was almost as far as from Wethersfield, to take the test. And apparently I did very well on the test because they accepted me at the University of Connecticut, but they said I would have to go to the Hartford branch.

For the next four years I went to school during the day and worked at night and on weekends. I worked at A.C. Peterson's as a soda jerk. I worked with my father on construction. I worked at a gas station. I worked at S.S. Pierce, an upscale food store. I worked for Allstate Insurance, doing filing and menial jobs. But between the $80 I got each month, which paid my rent, and these odd jobs, I was able to get along.

I got married in 1959, between my junior and senior year of college. I figured if my wife got pregnant I could still finish school before the baby was born. As it turned out, she didn't get pregnant for five years.

When I graduated I started going to law school at night, and I reversed everything. I worked during the day, and did a lot of construction work with my father. I liked seeing things built. Someteimes it was terrible. We worked in the wintertime. There's nothing colder than a house that's framed out but there's no heat inside. It's colder inside the house than it is outside.

I took a kind of weird journey in becoming a lawyer and an accountant. When I was stationed in California there was a community college. I wanted to take a course in chemistry because you needed chemistry for civil engineering. And a buddy of mine talked me into taking a marine biology course, so I never took chemistry. And that's the course I failed in my first year of college, because I didn't have that prerequeste. So I switched to the school of business and majored in accounting. And when I majored in accounting they had a business law and we studied the Constitution. I really got fascinated with the constitution and studying law, so I decided to take the LSATs.

I used to think I was pretty stupid, but when I passed the bar exam and the CPA exam in the same year I finally decided I'm not so stupid after all, and it completely reversed my thinking.

I started to think about writing a book about Mathew about ten years ago. As you get older, you start to think about the past. I thought about the last time Mathew came home. He got home very late. We knew he was coming so we left the house open. I was the only one up. It was about 2 o'clock in the morning. I had a bad toothache and couldn't sleep. So he stayed up with me, even though he was exhausted from the long trip. He told me what his plans were. He said, "You know, Betty's pregnant, and she's expecting around Christmastime. I've got to get a job when I get out of the service. I've got to finish school and then get a job. I have to take care of my family." He emphasized the word family. And Mathew was kind of a happy go lucky kid, good looking, had a lot of friends, female friends as well. He was all set to go back to school that September. He was going to get out in July or August. And of course the war started on June 25 and they froze his enlistment.

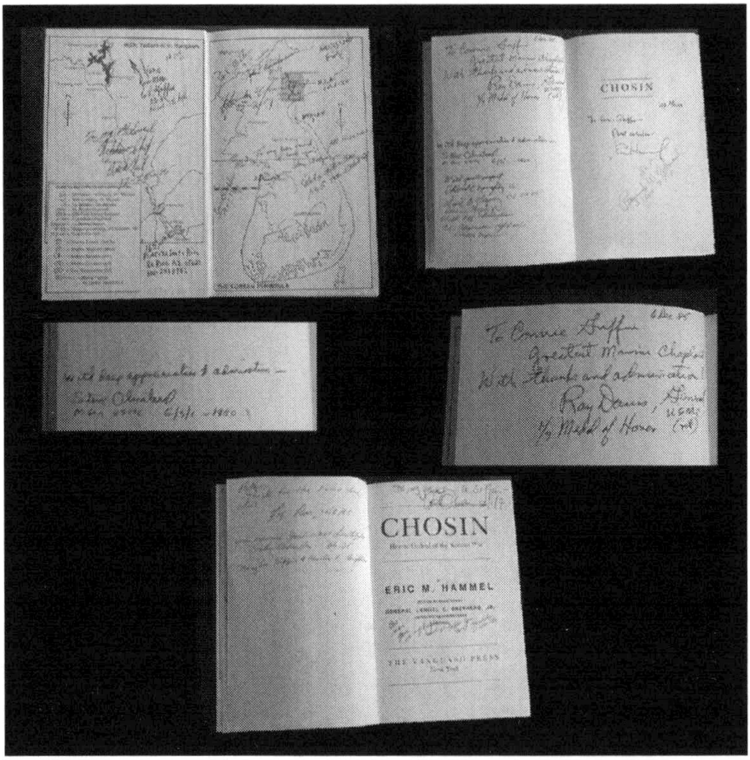

13 December 1944

"The book 'Chosin: Heroic Ordeal of the Korean War' was loaned to the chapel by Capt. Charles Griffin (retired)," Evan Adams wrote in a post on the Caruso Chapel Facebook page. "This book was originally a gift to Chaplain Cornelius Griffin, who later passed the book down to his nephew, Charles Griffin. The book was given to Chaplain Griffin in tribute to the events that transpired at the battle of the Chosin Reservoir. The book was written by Eric M. Hammel, with an introduction by General Lemuel C. Shepard, Jr. General Ray Davis (retired), who would later become assistant commandant of the Marine Corps, wrote of Chaplain Griffin as the greatest Marine chaplain. General Davis was one among many who signed the book before it was given to Chaplain Griffin."

Adams, a Seventh Day Adventist, is the command chaplain at the School of Infantry West, home of the Caruso Chapel at Camp Pendleton. He served two tours in Iraq, during which time young Marines died in his arms, and he organized a program whereby every Marine would get a cake on his birthday to share with other members of his squad or platoon.

As he leads a group of about 150 "Faith Warriors" wearing fatigues in a large auditorium on a Friday night before the rededication of the chapel in June of 2014, Adams shows slides of an aircraft carrier, a destroyer, other ships in the U.S. Navy. He beams a laser pointer to a large Naval gun and uses one of his favorite phrases to describe what it does. It "unleashes Hell," he says in a booming voice.

I'm sitting in a row near the back of the auditorium along with my brother Billy, himself a former Marine; his son Danny, who's a police detective in East Hartford, Conn.; Mathew's son Danny — although they are first cousins, this weekend is the first time the two Dannys have actually met — and my co-author, Aaron Elson. At the end of the program Adams introduces us and asks us to stand. As the Marines file out of the auditorium, one by one, every one of them passes by and shakes our hands.

Despite a sometimes troubled youth, Adams says, he knew from an early age that he wanted to be a chaplain. Adopted at birth, he never knew his biological parents, nor does he have any desire to find out about them.

"My dad was a World War II Marine," he said when I spoke with him on June 25, 2014, the day after the chapel's rededication. "When I was six years old we moved from New Jersey to New Hampshire. I spent most of my childhood there. I went to the Catholic church and went to St. Catherine's elementary school in Bedford, New Hampshire. I was a high school dropout. Actually I was expelled from school for some indiscretions. But then I got my graduate equivalency degree in 1990 and then went to Southern Adventist University in Collegedale, Tennessee, and graduated there with a triple major in 1994."

The majors, he says, were religion, health care administration and business administration.

"I was adopted at birth," he says, "so I did not realize that my parents were not my biological parents until they told me in about 1982. I was ten or eleven years old when they told me. They were the only parents I knew, so as a child it really didn't matter that much to me. I was home with a family that loved me and cared for me.

"I never tried to find my biological parents. I felt that my mother — when I say my mother I'm referring to my biological mother — made a very controversial choice, especially in the early 1970s when there was Roe v. Wade and woman's right to choose, she made a very brave decision to bear me, to endure the pregnancy, and then made a very brave choice and a responsible choice, which was 'I cannot provide for this child; I would like to adopt him out to someone who can.' So I respect her privacy.

"In ministry I have met people that have pursued finding out the whole adoption where did I come from thing, and it hasn't always worked out, because sometimes people will say 'Well, look, I made a choice those years ago and I moved on with my life, and I'm asking you to respect my privacy now.' So I chose to withhold any type of pursuing it to respect her privacy.

"Certainly if she ever came looking for me I'd be happy to acknowledge her and tell her my story, but I think for me to pursue it is the wrong thing. I just feel that way myself, that I want to respect her privacy and the decision she made."

Adams says it was his father who inspired him to go into the ministry.

"My dad was a World War II United States Marine," he says, "and he was in the Pacific along with all the other Marines, and they had to do some horrific things out there. And my dad, he was an alcoholic, and I think that by what he told me, drinking was a way of escape, to escape the horrific things that happened during the war.

"I can remember my dad telling me a story about when he was on a ship, the date was 13 December 1944, and he used to like to go out to the bow of the ship and watch the sun break the horizon. And one day, on 13 December 1944, while he was out there he noticed a black dot in the sky. He pulled out his spectacles and realized that that was an enemy plane and it was loaded with bombs. It was a kamikaze on a one-way mission. And the primary mission of the cruiser that he was stationed on was to protect the carrier at all costs, and so the horn for battle stations sounded, and he strapped himself in his dual .40s and he said, 'Son, we unleashed Hell.' And he said they laid a spray of cover fire in front of the carrier to protect the carrier. Well, the pilot made the escort the target so instead of ramming the carrier he rammed the cruiser, and he said, 'Son, there was an explosion and there was fire and smoke.' And he said, 'My best friend, Kevin, was stationed back there in a turret astern near the impact,' and so he unharnessed himself and ordered another Marine to take his place and he started to run down there and he began to splash on the deck, and he said 'Son, I couldn't believe it. We're way up here on the deck line and we're already getting seawater.' He looked down at the sole of his boot and it wasn't seawater. It was pools of human blood. He began to run further astern and he began to trip over debris on the deck and he said 'Son, I looked down and there were the dismemberments of sailors and Marines and they were dead, laying on the deck, and there were arms and legs and decapitations and all kinds of horrific things.' And he got back as close as he could, he said the fire was too hot, the smoke was too thick, and damage control was out there trying to put out the fire, and he said, 'Son, it didn't matter because Kevin's turret had been totally obliterated in the explosion.' He said, 'Son, I just began to run myself all the way around and I would pick somebody up but they were already dead, and i looked in the distance,' and he said, 'Son, I saw someone lying flat on their back, and their arms were flailing around,' and he ran over there and he grabbed his hand. It was like a cooked chicken wing, and the smell of burning flesh, if you've evere smelled burning flesh that's not a smell you soon forget. And he said, 'Son,' he looked down, he couldn't believe it. It was Kevin. And his eyes are rolled back in his head, he's in shock I guess, I mean I'm not a doctor, he said he's in shock, and Daddy said, 'Son, I did all I knew to do. I looked right in his face and yelled "KEVIN!"' And Daddy told me, 'Son, when I yelled at Kevin he snapped out of it and our eyes met, and he looked up at me,' and he said, 'Kevin said these words: "Gun. I knew you'd come. Gun. I knew you'd come." And he kept saying over and over again. "Gun. I knew you'd come." And Daddy said, 'Son, I thought he was gonna die right there on the deck.' So he scooped him up in his arms and he carried him down to sick bay, and as he was going, Kevin's arm dismembered from his body just like a Thanksgiving turkey leg on

Thanksgiving Day. And there were some sailors and Marines down there in sick bay. They were yelling for their mothers, they were yelling for Jesus, they were yelling for whoever they thought was listening to them.' And he said, 'Son, there was a dead sailor laying there on the rack but I took Kevin and I scooped him up and put him down there but Kevin had already died.'

"In all there were 330 souls, 330 that were either killed or wounded in the kamikaze attack of 13 December 1944 on the USS Nashville. And when my dad told me these stories, it seemed to give him a degree of peace, some sense of closure, that he could tell these stories, someone would listen, and someone would be interested and care enough to provide support, and at a very early age I realized that I had a gift. People would tell me things, and after they would talk to me about it, they would feel better. And as a very young person it's hard to understand at the time, but then I realized that I want to help American service members heal from their moral wounds, so that's why I joined the United States Navy Chaplain Corps. When I was ten years old I knew I wanted to be a chaplain in the United States Navy."

Marines on the march during the breakout from the Chosin Reservoir.

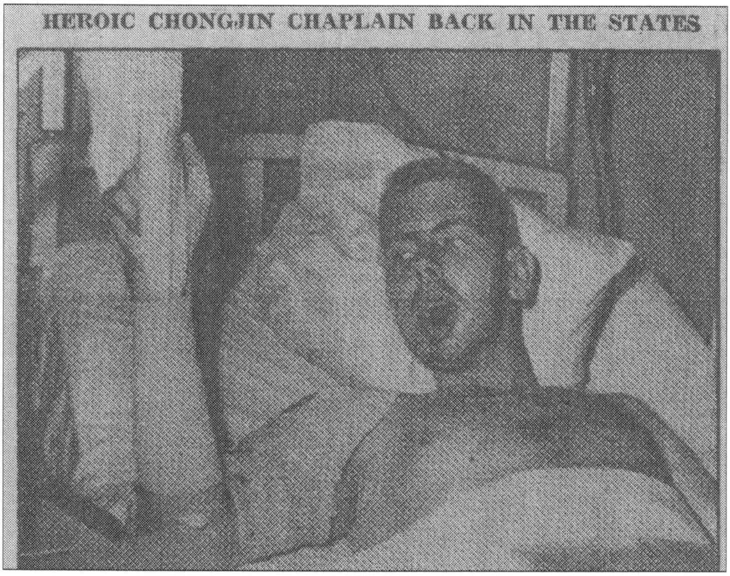
HEROIC CHONGJIN CHAPLAIN BACK IN THE STATES

Father Griffin in the hospital after being wounded.

Charles "Chip" Griffin, Msgr. Griffin's nephew. *(Photo by Marine Sgt. Christopher Duncan)*

The display about Mathew at Bulkeley High School. *(Photo by Aaron Elson)*

Mathew, left, Theresa and John Caruso. Our older brother George is behind Theresa. *(Caruso family photo)*

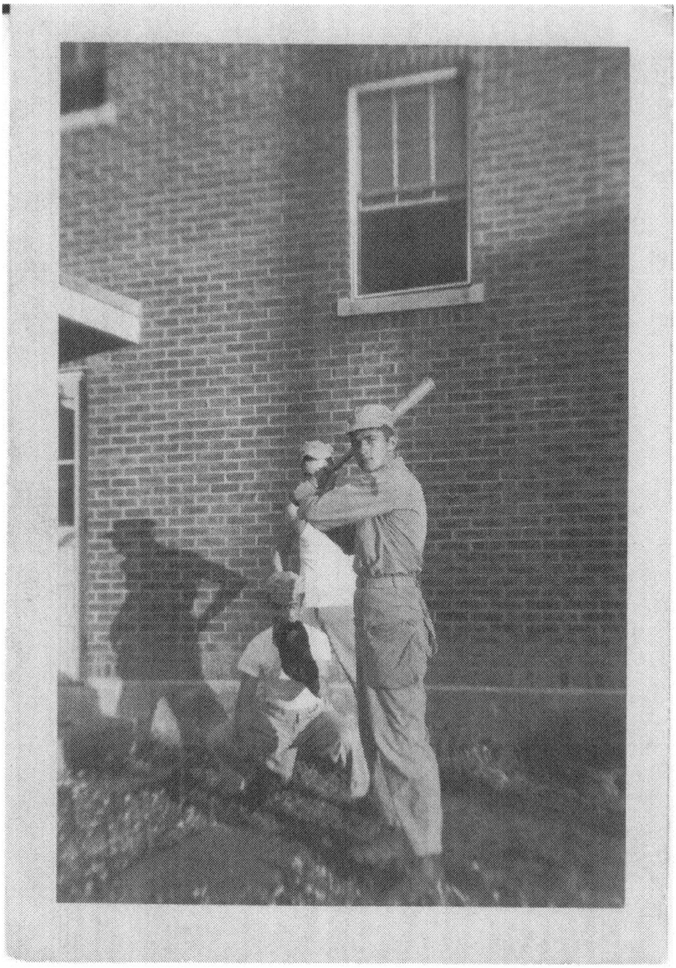

Mathew at Parris Island. *(Caruso family photo)*

CARUSO. In Manchester. Michael J. Caruso Sr. of 68 Cannon Road, East Hartford, husband of the late Harriet (Parnell) Caruso, died Saturday (June 20) at Manchester Memorial Hospital. He was born in Castel Franco Benevento, Italy, coming to Meriden when he was two years old. He attended schools in Meriden and had lived in Tarrytown, N.Y., before moving to Hartford 35 years ago. He was a gold star father of the Korean conflict. He was a member of the Royal Order of Moose. He was the oldest active member of Carpenters Local 43. He was a former president of the Carpenters Local 43 and a charter member of Barry Square Senior Citizens. He was a well-known builder in the area, having built many custom homes and commercial buildings. He was superintendent of construction of Constitution Plaza, The Travelers Insurance Cos. and the Hartford Insurance Group. He was a former Connecticut amateur featherweight and bantamweight boxing champion. He had played football for the Meriden West Ends. In 1912, he finished seventh in the Boston Marathon. He was a candidate with Jim Thorpe for the U.S. Olympic team in 1912. He leaves six sons, Michael J. Caruso of Hartford, Pat Caruso of Newington, attorney John Caruso of Farmington, Ralph Caruso of Manchester, Peter Caruso of Windsor and William Caruso of East Hartford; a daughter, Mrs. Lucille Brooks of East Hartford; a brother, Rocco Caruso of Carls Springs, Fla.; a sister, Rose Johnson of Raleigh, N.C.; 32 grandchildren, and 10 great-grandchildren. The funeral will be Tuesday, 9:15 a.m, from Farley-Sullivan Funeral Home, 96 Webster St., Hartford, followed by a mass of Christian burial, 10 a.m., at St. Augustine Church. Burial will be in Mount St. Benedict Cemetery, Bloomfield. Friends may call at the funeral home today, 7-9 p.m., and Monday, 2-4 and 7-9 p.m.

Mathew's father's obituary

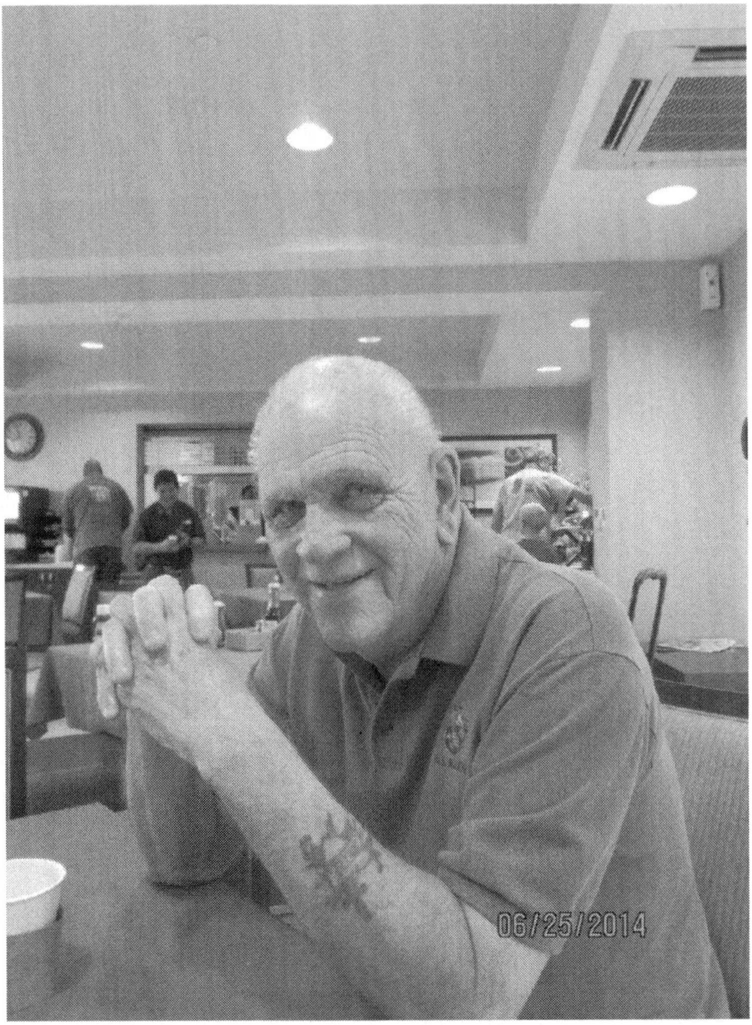

Bill Caruso, the youngest of the 10 Caruso siblings and himself a former Marine, at the chapel rededication.

From left, John Caruso, Dan Caruso, LCDR Evan Adams, Chip Griffin.

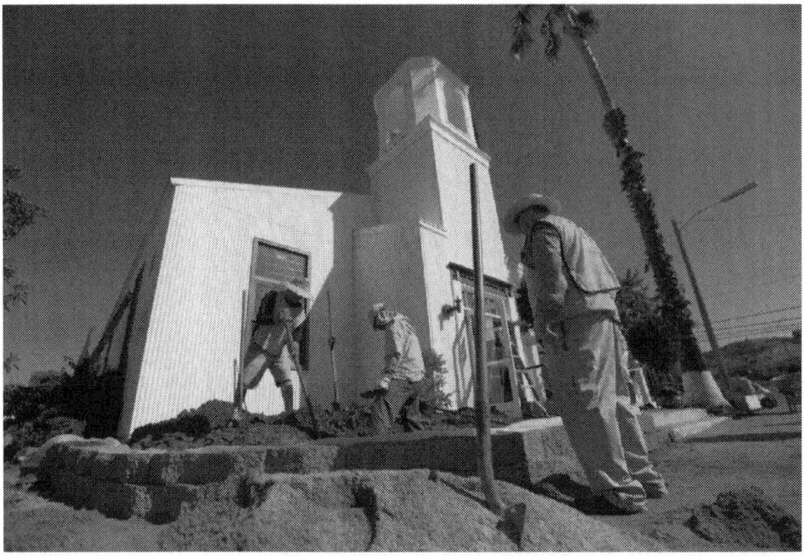

The chapel being refurbished by volunteers from the Church of Latter Day Saints.

(Marine Corps photo by Cpl. Michelle S. Brinn)

John Caruso beside a picture in the chapel of himself and Father Griffin.

(Marine Corps photo by Sgt. Christopher Duncan

Local Marine Died Heroically in Korea

Priest Says Sgt. Caruso Was Killed Shielding Him from Machine Gun Fire

A young Hartford Marine, who was killed in Korea Dec. 6, died a hero's death, it was learned today.

The Associated Press reported that Sgt. Matthew Caruso, 20, was killed by enemy machine-gun fire while trying to shield a Navy chaplain during the gallant retreat of the First Marine Division from the Chosin Reservoir.

The AP report today described how the Catholic chaplain, under whom Caruso served, received consolation from a Baptist chaplain who believed he was dying.

* * *

LT. CORNELIUS J. GRIFFIN told the Associated Press that he was giving last rites to Caruso in early December after machine-gun fire had riddled an ambulance. Caruso had thrown himself between the ambulance and the enemy fire in an attempt to save the priest's life.

The priest, however, was hit while bending over the fallen youth. His jaw and right arm were shattered and he believed he was dying. A Baptist chaplain H. Craven, noting the severe wounds, knelt beside Griffin and read the Catholic prayer of contrition.

Father Griffin said, "As long as we have comradeship like that, America will never lose."

* * *

SERGEANT CARUSO had written a letter to his father, Michael J. Caruso of 73 Webster St., shortly before he died. In it, he said, "I am confident that some day I will come back to all of you. I have an awful lot to live for—there will be my wife and baby waiting for me when I get back to the States."

His wife, the former Elizabeth Russell of 21 Washington St., Rocky Hill, gave birth to a son just six days after her husband was killed.

He also told his father, "I do know that I will be one of the many guys aboard ship heading back home when it is all over."

* * *

AND THEN he told of the close

SGT. MATTHEW CARUSO

friendship that had grown between him and the Catholic chaplain, which ultimately led to his heroic death. "I still am working for a chaplain," he said, "only this time it is a Catholic priest I am with. He really is a wonderful man and we get along fine. Every day when it is possible he says Mass for his boys and I have seen him give Holy Communion and administer the last rites under heavy machine gun fire by the enemy."

The sergeant had attended Bulkeley High School for three years and then enlisted in the Marines. He was married early in 1950 and left for Korea with the Seventh Regiment, First Marine Division, in August, 1950.

His wife and six-month-old son are living in Rocky Hill.

Caruso's Buddy Visits Widow; Was Near as Korea Hero Fell

Richard A. Roden, 21, son of Mrs. M. J. Armstrong, 197 Collins St., was only a few feet away from his buddy, Marine Sgt. Matthew Caruso, when a burst from

R. A. Roden

a spray gun killed Caruso and wounded the chaplain whose aide he was.

Roden hadn't said much about Caruso's death until he saw Monday night's Times. On Page One was the chaplain's story of "Mickey" Caruso's death. On Monday evening, Roden went to Rocky Hill to talk to Caruso's young widow and console her. "Mickey died quick," he said. "He didn't have time to feel pain."

Roden, home for a few days' leave, is a hospitalman in the Navy. He was attached to the Marine outfit in which Caruso was a chaplain's assistant. On Dec. 6, 1950, the Marines were retreating from the Chosin Reservoir.

* * *

"I HAD JUST brought a wounded man to an ambulance," Roden said today, "when a bur[illegible] gun sprayed the area. I went b[illegible] for another wounded man and brought him to the ambulance. It was then that a chief pharmacist's mate told me my buddy had been killed while I was standing outside a few minutes earlier.

"The slug that killed him went right through the folded hands of a man the chaplain was praying over. The chaplain (Lt. Cornelius J. Griffin, a Catholic priest) got hit in the jaw. He's still in tough shape. I saw him in a hospital in Oakland and he couldn't talk very well."

* * *

RODEN met Caruso once or twice in Hartford before leaving Hartford Public High School to enlist in the Navy in 1947. Two weeks before Caruso's death they met again in Korea, and the two men and the chaplain became close friends.

Roden has been wounded twice, once in the foot by a bullet and once in the arm and side by shrapnel. He has refused a medical discharge, but says he is suffering from battle fatigue. He is at home on a short leave.

Two articles from my sister Lucille's scrapbook.

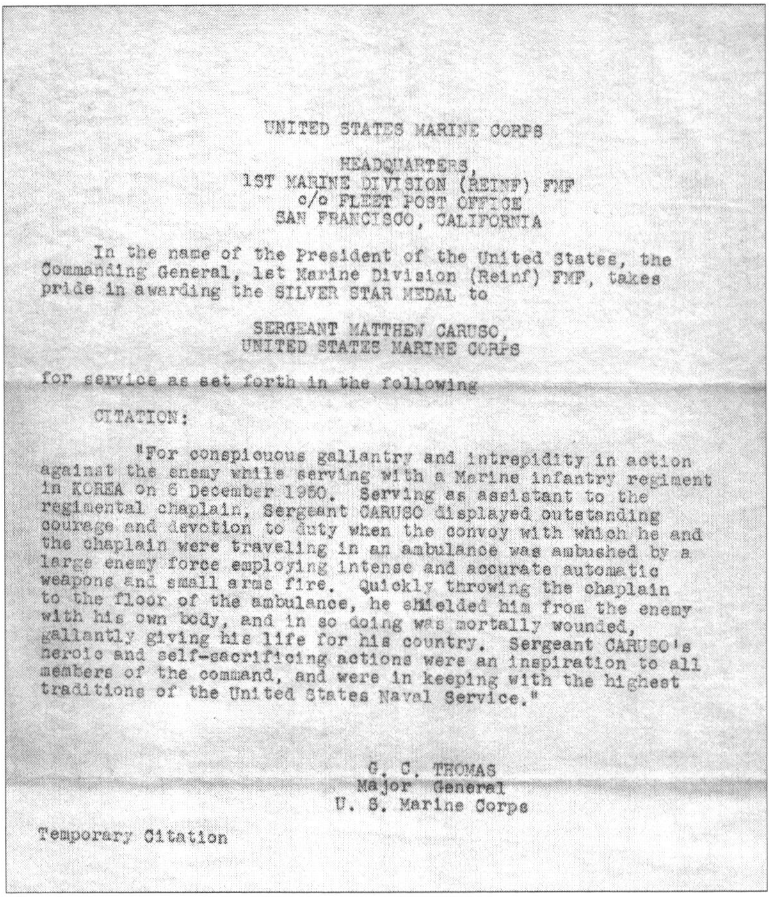

UNITED STATES MARINE CORPS

HEADQUARTERS,
1ST MARINE DIVISION (REINF) FMF
c/o FLEET POST OFFICE
SAN FRANCISCO, CALIFORNIA

In the name of the President of the United States, the Commanding General, 1st Marine Division (Reinf) FMF, takes pride in awarding the SILVER STAR MEDAL to

SERGEANT MATTHEW CARUSO,
UNITED STATES MARINE CORPS

for service as set forth in the following

CITATION:

"For conspicuous gallantry and intrepidity in action against the enemy while serving with a Marine infantry regiment in KOREA on 6 December 1950. Serving as assistant to the regimental chaplain, Sergeant CARUSO displayed outstanding courage and devotion to duty when the convoy with which he and the chaplain were traveling in an ambulance was ambushed by a large enemy force employing intense and accurate automatic weapons and small arms fire. Quickly throwing the chaplain to the floor of the ambulance, he shielded him from the enemy with his own body, and in so doing was mortally wounded, gallantly giving his life for his country. Sergeant CARUSO's heroic and self-sacrificing actions were an inspiration to all members of the command, and were in keeping with the highest traditions of the United States Naval Service."

G. C. THOMAS
Major General
U. S. Marine Corps

Temporary Citation

Mathew's Silver Star citation. Note the "temporary" status.

Korea Front 'Fairly Quiet' But Winsted Sergeant Dies

WINSTED, April 14 (Special)— A Winsted soldier serving in Korea on April 2 wrote home to his folks that it was "fairly quiet" in his sector. Three days later he was killed in combat.

The Department of Defense on Monday notified Mr. and Mrs. William H. Caine of 175 N. Main St. of the death on April 5 of their son, Master Sergeant Edward Harry Caine. He would have been 21 years old May 7.

The youth's father, a veteran of World War I, suffered machine-gun wounds in the arms and legs and was gassed at Verdun, France, Sept. 8, 1918.

In his last letter to his parents Sgt. Caine said the "Commies are probing but have been thrown back." In mentioning a check he had sent his mother, he told her "to buy shoes or anything else you need." He added, "That's an order because I am now a platoon leader."

Mrs. Caine said Monday that in another letter Sgt. Caine said he always thanked God when he and his men got back safely. Her nephew, Matthew Caruso, son of Michael J. Caruso and the late Mrs. Hattie Caruso of Hartford, was killed Dec. 6, 1950 in Korea.

M. SGT. EDWARD CAINE

Cousin

Winsted Soldier Who Gave Life Halting Reds Gets Silver Star

Special to The Hartford Times

With the 3d Infantry Division in Korea. The Silver Star has been awarded posthumously to a Winsted, Conn., soldier killed in action last April.

He is M/Sgt. Edward H. Caine, son of Mr. and Mrs. William H. Caine of 175 North Main St., Winsted, and brother of Mrs. Mable K. Copping of 254 Albany Ave., Hartford. He earned the decoration Apr. 5 near Chunggo pan when a reinforced enemy company attacked the defensive positions in his area of the 3d Infantry Division front.

* * *

THE CITATION, in part, said, "Although he was painfully wounded, Sergeant Caine manned the machine-gun of a wounded man and ordered him evacuated." He then spotted a group of Communists making a hole in the barbed wire fence surrounding the company area. He ordered his men to hold fire until the enemy presented a more profitable target.

"As the hostile troops began moving through the opening in the fence, he laid down such devastating fire that numerous casualties were inflicted and the foe withdrew.

* * *

WHEN the Reds again tried to charge through the hole in the fence, Caine had left his machine gun to help a wounded comrade.

"Taking the weapon of the wounded man, he fearlessly dashed over the fire-swept terrain to a position where he could fire most effectively on the assaulting foe.

"Although this position was completely exposed to the hostile fire, he undauntedly remained, firing with such accuracy that the enemy was forced to flee in disorder.

"Seeing the enemy assault repulsed, he proceeded to leave his hazardous position, but in doing so he was mortally wounded by an enemy mortar blast."

A Star of Silver for a Golden Deed

FOR BRAVERY — The family of Master Sgt. Edward H. Caine receives the silver star he earned in Korea when, despite his own wounds, he went to the aid of a wounded buddy and was killed. Left to right: Col. Frederick J. [illegible], reading the citation; Mrs. Theodore [illegible], sister; [illegible], niece; Theodore [illegible]; William G. Caine, brother, and parents, Mr. and Mrs. William H. Caine.—Times Photo.

Mathew wasn't the only Korean War hero from the Caruso family. My cousin, Ed Caine, also lost his life and was awarded a posthumous Silver Star.

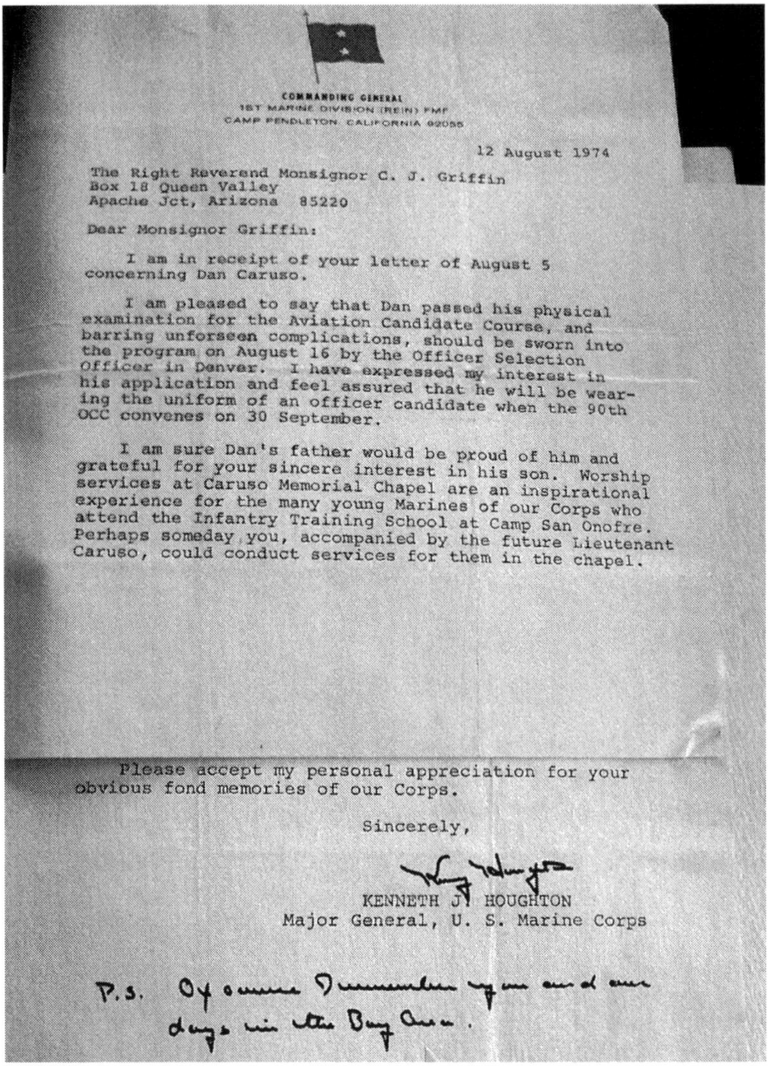

COMMANDING GENERAL
1ST MARINE DIVISION (REIN) FMF
CAMP PENDLETON, CALIFORNIA 92055

12 August 1974

The Right Reverend Monsignor C. J. Griffin
Box 18 Queen Valley
Apache Jct, Arizona 85220

Dear Monsignor Griffin:

I am in receipt of your letter of August 5 concerning Dan Caruso.

I am pleased to say that Dan passed his physical examination for the Aviation Candidate Course, and barring unforseen complications, should be sworn into the program on August 16 by the Officer Selection Officer in Denver. I have expressed my interest in his application and feel assured that he will be wearing the uniform of an officer candidate when the 90th OCC convenes on 30 September.

I am sure Dan's father would be proud of him and grateful for your sincere interest in his son. Worship services at Caruso Memorial Chapel are an inspirational experience for the many young Marines of our Corps who attend the Infantry Training School at Camp San Onofre. Perhaps someday you, accompanied by the future Lieutenant Caruso, could conduct services for them in the chapel.

Please accept my personal appreciation for your obvious fond memories of our Corps.

Sincerely,

KENNETH J. HOUGHTON
Major General, U. S. Marine Corps

P.S. Of course I remember you and our days in the Bay Area.

Major Gen. Ken Houghton's letter to Msgr. Griffin.

SAR plays vital role in local rescue work

By LCpl. Julius Moore Jr.

Winds blowing through cold mountain passes—roads icy and slick—California weather at its worst and when four men in a four-wheeler set out to challenge nature fate seems frozen in the balance.

Their vehicle hits a patch of ice and slides into an embankment, rolls over and down an 800 foot gorge.

Serious injury and even death may greet them on this cold Christmas night.

The above scenario is true. It did happen. And the call went out for the Marines.

Answering the call was El Toro's Search and Rescue team. Four men were stranded at the bottom of an almost inaccessable ravine in the Saddleback Mountains, about nine miles northeast of El Toro.

The four man SAR team consisted of pilot, Capt. Daniel Caruso, co-pilot, Capt. Doug Morgan, crew chief, Cpl. Leo Bottella and HM3 Don Willey.

Describing the accident Caruso said, "Road conditions were pretty bad. The four men were traveling down an icy road when their vehicle ran into a steep embankment and overturned into the ravine."

Caruso continued, "OCFD did most of the work. All we did was drop our hoist and the corpsman rappeled down to bring the four men up from the ravine. In the process Willey had to give one of the men medical attention before we could bring him up. There was one fatality. Two of the three survivors were transported to Mission Community Hospital in Mission Viejo.

Even though Search and Rescue's primary mission is to support 3d MAW'S tactical aircraft, they provided life saving assistance to the Orange County Fire Department by flying 25 rescue missions in 1981 alone.

The Orange County Fire Department (OCFD) only calls for assistance from the Marines in extreme emergencies such as when a helicopter and hoist are needed, or if for some reason OCFD lacks adequate back up support.

Jim Radley, Orange County assistant fire chief, feels the support SAR provides them is vital to their operations. "We don't have a helicopter and hoist at our immediate disposal. When SAR flies in with their four man team, they're ready to perform a service that otherwise might not be available to us. The turn around time is about one hour or less from the time they first receive our call. They're outstanding."

SAR has distinguished themselves with an outstanding record of successful rescue missions. Willey was awarded a Medal of Valor from the Irvine Lions' Club last March for his effort in a resuce mission in Riverside County in rough terrain.

And recently Morgan was awarded a Certificate of Commendation by the Orange County Board of Supervisors for his work as a member of SAR since 1978.

"In a critical situation, when every minute counts, SAR can transport patients to the nearest hospital in five to seven minutes. Transporting patients by ambulance might take three times as long," Radley said.

An article about Dan Caruso's work as a Marine helicopter rescue pilot.

Dan in 1984

John Caruso and tournament director Jeff Lee, right, present Debra Rothstein of the Hartford Foundation for Public Giving with a check for $3,000 raised during the first annual Mathew Caruso Memorial Scholarship Fund Golf Tournament.

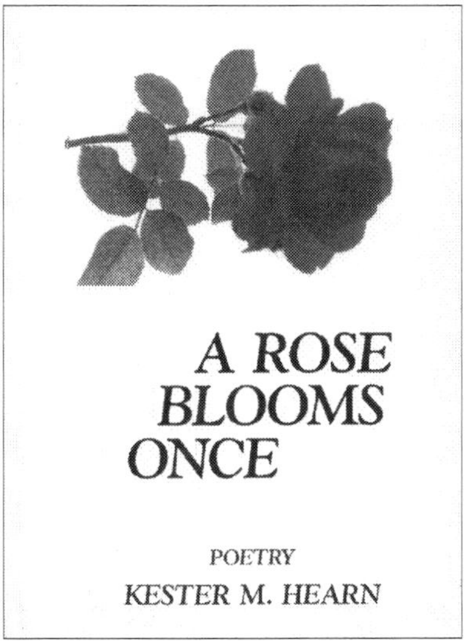

The Third Chaplain

According to the Navy Chaplain Corps history, there were three chaplains with the 7th Regiment as the Marines marched north: Chaplain Craven, Father Griffin, and Kester Hearn, a Methodist.

Chaplain Hearn was a decade older than Father Griffin, having been born in 1908, which would have made him 42 in 1950. Like Griffin he grew up on a farm, in Oklahoma rather than Indiana. After the Korean War he was a minister at the First United Methodist Church in Fort Worth, Texas, until his retirement. He passed away 1996.

I was unable to locate any family members, and the current leaders of the First United Methodist Church where he served as pastor couldn't tell me anything about Hearn, but I was able to find online a book that he wrote, and ordered the sole remaining available used copy.

At first I was a disappointed, as I expected a memoir with a gripping account of his time in Korea. Instead, "A Rose Blooms Once" was a book of poetry Hearn self-published after he retired. And most of the poems were about growing up on a farm, about his cat, about God, some limericks even. And then I found it: a section of poems titled "War — Absurd! Absurd!"

The section had only four poems, each of which was followed by a brief commentary. Today it seems odd to see a man of the cloth refer to an enemy combatant as a "gook," but that's what we called them during the Korean War.

Dumb, smoking steel monster

Dumb, smoking steel monster — It's done!
It knows not what's done, nor cares.
The recoil returns, the smoke curls down.
Beyond a mountain a flash is seen
Fifteen seconds counted — three miles away
it's done!

Words cannot tell but It's done!
God's choicest handiwork who breathed
Loved and were loved lie scattered on the ground.
Load in charges "six and seven," reach out
Ten thousand yards away the thunder says again
it's done!

When will God's will reach out and
be done
Beyond the mountains and every sea?
And the smoke cease curling from this thing's
unfeeling throat
And men rise above their ancient ways
To Christ — and loving wisdom in every heart
be done?

"I began this poem, Dumb, Smoking, Steel Monster," Hearn writes in his commentary, "while resting in the 121st Army Evacuation Hospital at Hungnam, Korea, on November 7, 1950. It reflects what I saw and experienced on November 4. We had moved a few miles north of the third water power station from the Chosin Reservoir, and spent the night in a Gook mud hut. Our artillery was nearby and fired all night, shaking dirt from the ceiling. The water in our canteens froze solid that night. The "Dumb, Smoking Steel Monsters" were our own 105 Howitzers. After each firing, as the barrel of the 105 slowly slid back to position, the smoke — lazily — idiotically — curled out the muzzle and down the muzzle. It appeared so dumb and unutterably stupid! From flash time to report time and multiplying by 1,100 feet I roughly knew the distance shot. Charges "six and seven" meant the weight of powder used, and distance shot. This is my first poem; and I worked on it many hours aboard ship while I was coming back to the States."

War is Such a Lovely Thing

(My experience as a chaplain in the Korean War — 1950-52)

He gazed at me with glassy eye
As my battalion and I passed by.
In that clobbered town he sat
With burned legs crossed, and leaning back
Following a napalm bomb attack.
Dead and swollen there he sat
Naked — roasted — bloody — black
His buddies nearby in a stack
A gruesome scene, intense the stink,
Autumn trees lay among the foes
Wisps of smoke still slowly rose.

Somewhere back home this word would go
"It is with regret that we report
Your son — your husband —,
Daddy Ling his ID says,
Was killed in action ten days ago."
His children do not understand
Why they'll never see their Dad again.
Thirty-three years have passed that day
Yet memory forbids him go away.
Ling still sits there by that tree
His glassy eyes still fixed on me.

To militarism the world must cling
War is such a lovely thing.

Hearn's comment: "Just after breakfast, August 9, 1985, I was thinking about the Korean War. As the 1st Battalion, 7th Regiment, 1st Marine Division, of which I was chaplain (Padre, they called me), was moving north, we came to the third hydro-electric power plant south of the Chosin Reservoir. Here we passed through a devastated town; and here I saw the burned, blacked and swollen North Korean or Chinese soldier sitting on folded legs, slightly leaning back. His glassy eyes were fixed on me and all who passed by. I was thinking of this gruesome scene when the thought came to me, "War is such a lovely thing." And this last line of the poem became its beginning and its title. Finished August 11, 1986. Written 33 years after the War."

My brother Mathew sacrificed his life to save Father Griffin. Yet he didn't willingly give his life like you'd put a five dollar bill in the collection plate on Sunday. He didn't have time to think about all the dreams he had about becoming a father and furthering his education and getting a job and buying a house and raising a family before he threw Father Griffin on the floor of the ambulance and shielded the padre with his body, yet he knew full well the consequence of his action. That's why this third poem by Chaplain Hearn, the first in his section on the Korean War, affects me so deeply. The Ed in the poem didn't give his life for his country, the way we hear at Memorial Day programs and in so many Facebook tributes, but rather he had his life taken violently away, in all likelihood without having had the option of ducking or the time to dive into a foxhole, whereas Mathew knowingly sacrificed his life, as in the passage from the Bible that goes: "Greater love has no man than this, that a man lay down his life for his friends. "

The Home Coming

Ed's orders read, "You will report
for active duty on August four."
He kissed his wife, his daughter, son
and held them tightly one by one.
When time ran out he waved "Goodbye"

as long and far as he could see.
His family's future was rosy, bright,
big things they'd planned after the fight.
With pack on back he boarded ship
and sailed on his far distant trip.

He disembarked on day sixteen
in a foreign land he'd never seen.
He never had hunted or owned a gun
now over his shoulder an M-1 slung.
He saddled up for the front line
ignorant of all the hell he'd find
Ed's hopes were high that Autumn day
the War, he thought, would go his way
And very soon he would return
to his family, his first concern.

Short hours before sunset that day
on bloody soil the soldier lay
A shrapnel slug had zeroed in
and blew away his face and brain.
From empty skull I hid my face
savage, brutal, mankind's disgrace.
The patriots who ordered him to fight,
ten thousand miles from this sight,
Dined in the Congressional Dining Hall
on gourmet food before their Ball.

By dog-tag Ed was identified
and by two pictures at his side
A picture of his precious Three
the other, where he longed to be.
He returned home in a sealed casket
with his headless body neatly in it.
Ed was met by broken hearts and streams
of tears and shattered dreams.
A Chaplain prayed, then Taps was heard
"He gave his life??" Absurd! Absurd!

"I came upon this Marine (Ed) soon after he had been killed," Hearn wrote. "All but a little of the back of his skull had been blown away. That sight still hurts me to this day. As chaplain it was my job to write to the next of kin. A sad job. I began this poem November 17, 1985; completed it April 15, 1988. No, he did not give his life. He wanted to live as much as anyone. It was violently taken from him."

A WW2 Battle Fought With Coffee Cups

Bulkeley High School also had its share of students who fought in Korea as well as in Vietnam and subsequent wars.

One who served in Korea was Joseph Hendron of Wethersfield, Connecticut, who knew the Carusos growing up.

"I was born in Hartford," Hendron said during an interview in 2014. "I lived on the street next to the Carusos, and knew Mike more than any of them. Matty was younger than me. I'm shooting at 85 now.

"I think there were about eight kids in the family. I knew their father was a builder. I don't remember their mother."

Hendron's father, like the elder Caruso, was a builder as well. "He built the house I was born in," Hendron said, "a beautiful house. They lost the house in the Depression, and everything went down the tubes. We had to move into a three-family house. Then he pulled himself up and became the manager of Brainard Field Airport. He was 53 when he died. My father died, and two months later my brother joined the Navy during World War II." (Interestingly, Mathew joined the Marines following his mother's death in 1947.)

While Mike Caruso was a Navy corpsman, Frank Hendron, Joe's older brother, became a signalman on the destroyer escort USS Buckley. Interviewed for the newsletter at Avery Heights, the assisted living facility where he resides, Frank declined to talk about the war. But the USS Buckley was involved in one of the most unusual battles of World War II, a battle fought with coffee cups.

Just as the engagement in which Mathew was killed took place between midnight and 2 a.m., the battle between the Buckley and the German submarine U-66 occurred in the middle of the night. The Buckley was escorting the aircraft carrier USS Block Island on the night of May 6, 1944, on submarine patrol in the Atlantic when word came in from a spotter plane that a German submarine was sighted on the surface in the area. The Buckley was dispatched to locate it.

As the Buckley approached, barely coming into sight under the light of a bright moon, the sub remained on the surface, traveling in a circle.

The captain of the Buckley surmised the sub's captain might have thought the Buckley was a German refueling ship. The sub fired three red flares as a signal of recognition. The Buckley did not respond.

At 3:17 a.m., at a range of 4,000 yards, "personnel aft reported a torpedo wake passing down the starboard side," the Buckley's after action report, written on May 8, says. The ship altered course to keep the sub in the moonlight and avoid torpedoes. At 3:20, the order was given for the Buckley "to commence firing" at a range of 2,100 yards. "The very first salvo from the three-inch guns scored a direct hit on the sub's forecastle," the after action report says. The enemy had opened fire first with machine guns.

A furious battle ensued as the two ships jockeyed for position. The submarine was on the surface at all times, and soon it became clear the ships were trying to ram each other.

All the while, the pilot of a spotter plane from the Block Island was radioing back a play by play to the aircraft carrier, according to the after action report.

At 3:29 a.m., the Buckley, which had come alongside the submarine, "gives hard right rudder, rides up on the forecastle of sub and stays there," the report says. "Men begin swarming out of submarine and up on Buckley's forecastle. Machine gun, tommy gun, and rifle fire knocks off several. Ammunition expended at this time included several general mess coffee cups which were on hand at ready gun station. Two of the enemy were hit in the head with these. Empty shell cases were also used by crew of three-inch gun No. 2 to repel boarders. ... Buckley suffers only casualty of engagement when man bruises fist knocking one of enemy over the side. Several men, apparently dead, could be seen hanging over the side of the sub's bridge at this time. The boatswain's mate in charge of forward ammunition party kills a man, attempting to board, with a .45 pistol. Man falls back over side. Midships repair party equipped with rifles mans life lines and picks off several men on deck of submarine."

It should be noted that the coffee cups used in the battle were not made of styrofoam; nor were they the light aluminum or tin coffee cups that brought a measure of warmth to GIs in foxholes. No, sir. The Navy dines in style. These were heavy China coffee cups, and maybe even had an anchor emblem on the side. Getting hit in the head with one of these thrown with the speed and accuracy of a baseball could inflict a fair amount of damage.

"If it wasn't for those heavy coffee cups," Charles Harmon, who like Frank Hendron was a signalman third class on the Buckley, told the St. Petersburg Times in an article published Nov. 18, 1944, "we couldn't have kept the Germans from coming on the deck and would have had a bloody hand-to-hand battle."

According to Sharkhunters.com, a web site devoted to the history of the German U-boats, the battle between U-66 and the Buckley was the basis for the movie "The Enemy Below," starring Robert Mitchum and Kurt Jurgens as the two opposing captains, although the U-66 was never under the surface during the actual battle and the coffee cup scene was not in the picture. According to Sharkhunters, the movie had two different endings. In the one shown most often on television, after the battle in which the submarine is sunk, the two skippers are seen on the fantail of the American ship sharing a cigarette. In the other ending, both captains are killed when the U-boat explodes. In reality, the captain of U-66 was one of the submarine's 36 casualties, whereas the skipper of the Buckley, Lieutenant Commander Brent M. Abel, not only survived but was awarded the Navy Cross.

After the battle, the Buckley headed for New York to be repaired. Three weeks after the sinking of U-66, on May 29, 1944, the Block Island itself was struck by three torpedoes and sunk with the loss of six lives; more than 900 other crew men were rescued by other American ships.

The Carusos "were a family of Marines," Joe Hendron said. "They loved the Marine Corps. My wife and I were in California a few years back visiting our daughter, so while we were there we said, 'Let's go down to Camp Pendleton and see what it looks like.' It was totally changed from what I remember back in 1950. There was a nice main gate, and today you just drive in and out without any checking. When I was there in 1950 they had Tent Camp 1 and Tent Camp 2. I asked one of the guards, 'Where's Tent Camp 1?'

"He said, 'What's that? The only tents we have here is the Boy Scouts camping in the hills.'"

Mathew left Bulkeley High during his junior year and enlisted in the Marines. Hendron graduated three years later.

"There were six of us who graduated Bulkeley in 1950," Hendron said. "The war started in June, and we graduated in June. In September we went and joined up at the Hartford Post Office. So we all shipped out together from the Hartford railroad station to Yammassee, South Carolina. That was the receiving point for new recruits. And the minute you got off the train you knew you were in the Marine Corps because there was a big sergeant waiting for you.

"The ironic part is that everybody goes through the same thing. Guys before us and guys after us. The training never changes. It's probably different now. But our group, we had all the drill instructors from World War II, and they were hard-nosed. They had the combat experience, and when they came back they made them drill instructors. No nonsense. They were the type of guys that would pull you out at 2 o'clock in the morning and make you go back in and grab your mattress and pull your mattress out of the quonset hut.

"The six of us all stayed together, and somehow maneuvered our way to get into the same hut, so we could cry on each other's shoulders at night. After boot camp, though, we all separated, and four of us went to Camp Pendleton. We had the advanced training, boarded a ship, and we weren't in the Marine Corps that long before we were getting shot at. Young kids right out of high school, what are we doing here? We arrived in Korea at the end of March, and all those guys from the Chosin were coming back. We took a look at those guys and wondered, wow, is that what we're going to go through up there?"

Of the six who enlisted from Bulkeley, Hendron said, two were killed. And on Sept. 11, 1951, the other four from the group, although in different parts of Korea, were wounded on the same day.

"Four from the group," Hendron said, "that made the papers here."

On his way to Korea, Hendron said, "we hit a typhoon. Everybody was sick. This friend of mine that I graduated with and stayed with, he was in the bottom rack, and he couldn't go to the mess hall. I'd go to the mess hall and I'd come back and I'd see a hand come out from underneath the bunk. Just a hand. And I'd put an apple or a banana in it.

"Then we get to Pusan. They flew us up to the front lines, and we boarded big trucks and they drove us the rest of the way. Then they separate everybody. We were replacements. I went to Able Company and Bob Kelly, who was on the bottom rack, he went to Charlie Company, but we'd see each other occasionally because we'd come back for a rest. You're supposed to be 30 days up on the line and 15 days back for a rest, so when we'd come back for a rest everybody would be together.

"When I got wounded on September 11 I was coming down a hill and he was going up, and he went crazy. They said they had to restrain him and pull him back down again. He didn't get wounded, but psychologically he broke. The other two guys were wounded."

A few years ago, Hendron returned with his wife to Korea.

"What a difference," he said. "When we left Seoul it was a shambles. There was no Seoul. It was just a building here, a building there that was left standing. But you go back there now, all you see is high rises. And a big amusement park right in the center of the city. Mammoth hotels. Our flight was all paid for by the South Korean government, we only had to pay for half of my wife's flight over there. But once we got there, all the meals were free, nothing but the best, and nothing but thank you, thank America, thank you Marines."

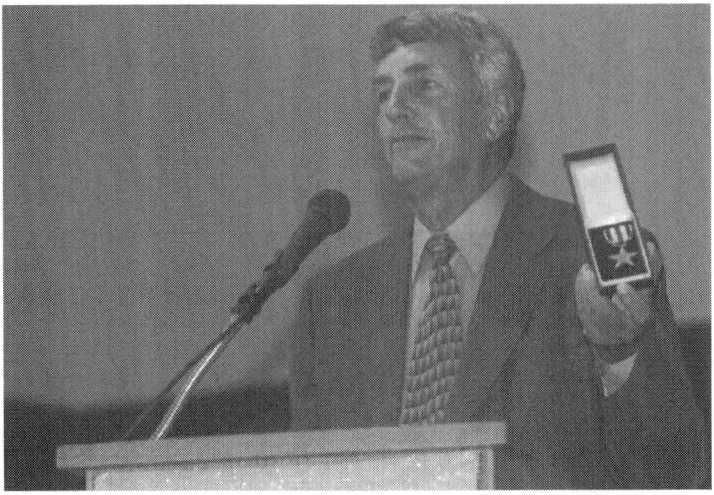

Dan Caruso with Mathew's Silver Star at the chapel rededication.

Marine Corps photo by Sgt. Christopher Duncan

"Youse People"

The Caruso Chapel was rededicated on June 23, 2014. My brother Billy, who lives in Arizona, was there along with his son Dan, a detective in East Hartford, Conn. Betty Smith, Mathew's widow, who lives in San Francisco, drove down with Dan, who came from Oregon. My co-author, Aaron Elson, was also there along with his sister, Bonnie Freeman, who lives in San Pedro, Calif., a couple of hours down the coast from Camp Pendleton.

I hadn't seen Betty or Dan since the funeral almost 60 years before, and Billy's son Dan had never met his cousin Dan, so the weekend was as much a reunion as it was a rededication.

The day after the rededication, Aaron and I were able to sit down with Betty and Dan and learn some of the details of their lives. What follows is an edited transcript of our conversation:

Aaron Elson: Betty, what was your maiden name?

Betty Smith: Russell.

Aaron: And you grew up in ...

Betty: Rocky Hill, Connecticut.

Dan Caruso: I was born in Hartford. I grew up as an Army brat and moved all around the States.

Aaron: How old are you now?

Dan: I'm 63.

Betty: I'm 83.

Aaron: How did you and Matt meet?

Betty: A friend of his gave him my phone number. He started calling me and we started talking on the phone. I don't remember the date we met. He was in the Marines then.

Aaron: And when were you married?

Betty: In May of 1950. We were only married a short time. I was working at the Travelers Insurance Company in Hartford in the steno department, and he found a place in somebody's back yard, a converted shed that had two little tiny apartments. I quit my job and went down there. I was there only six weeks when he was deployed.

Aaron: Tell me more about the apartment.

Betty: It was just a bedroom, a tiny kitchen, and bathroom. And they also had a couple living in their house. So they had two couples in the back yard and one couple in the house.

Aaron: Now you were pregnant, and Mathew was expecting to get out of the service?

Betty: I was totally shocked. The major that was in the next little apartment brought him home so he could say goodbye to me.

Aaron: Did Mathew write often once he was deployed?

Betty: Yes, he did. My mother told me to burn the letters or get rid of them because I would cry when I read them. That was after my second marriage. I used to have lots of nightmares then. I would dream that he came back, and everybody had seen him, but I didn't see him because I was married again. Although that was something he had told me he wanted me to do if anything happened to him. He said, "You're too young to live alone. I want you to get married again." But I still felt funny. I felt strange about it. I felt kind of guilty. My mother was interviewed when his body was brought back and she told the reporter that, and I was so angry when I read it. She said, "My daughter's going to be upset that I told you that." And it was in the newspaper that he had said that. Because I remember when John was there at the funeral, after the funeral we went to his father's house, and Father Griffin was there, and John brought that up, and Father Griffin said, "I almost got mad at him because he always said something was going to happen." It was like everybody knew something was going to happen. He had bought me an opal ring before he gave me the engagement ring, and there was a cross on the ring. It was a little black cross, there was nothing on the ring, it was just there. And my grandfather, my mother's father, said to my mother, "I hope she hurries up and has that baby before she gets bad news." And when I went back from North Carolina, my father met me and I said, "I'm never going to see him again."

Aaron: So not only you, but other people as well had some premonition that something would, happen to Matt.

Betty: Yes. And Father Griffin said that Matt talked about it a lot, that he wouldn't be coming back. I didn't feel that way. When I was pregnant and I was living with my mother, I didn't feel that he was not coming back. I would cut out of the newspaper every day any article about Korea.

Aaron: At the time he was killed, there were articles in the newspaper about the Marines breaking out of the Chosin Reservoir. So did you think that he was safe?

Betty: No. Because once the Chinese entered, before that I thought he'd be home by Christmas, but then the Chinese came into the war.

Aaron: How did you learn of Mathew's death?

Betty: By telegram. On the 19th of December. Dan has the telegram. The man that brought the telegram was a local man that ran the telegraph station, and he told my grandfather that he waited as long as he could at night to bring it; he just dreaded bringing it. So it came kind of late at night.

Aaron: And it was Christmastime. Was the house decorated?

Betty: Probably. We always had a Christmas tree. But I don't remember it.

Aaron: How did your family come to live in Rocky Hill?

Betty: My grandfather owned a house. It was built in 1900. They lived in East Hartford and Hartford, then they moved to Rocky Hill. And my father lived in Cromwell. His parents lived on a tobacco farm.

Aaron: Does your family go back many generations?

Betty: My mother's family came on the Mayflower.

Aaron: And what was the name of your ancestor?

Betty: We're descended from two of them. Isaac Allerton, and, oh, gee, what's the other name? I have two authenticated names from the Mayflower Society. I'm a member of that.

Dan: There was a children's book that came out years ago ["Three Young Pilgrims," by Cheryl Harness], that talked about a little girl ...

Betty: Mary Allerton.

Dan: That was the main character of the book. She's one of our ancestors.

Betty: She was the last survivor of the Mayflower. And she married Thomas Cushman, who was the business manager for the Mayflower, but he didn't come on the Mayflower because when the other ship went back, he and his son went back. But Mary Allerton did come on the Mayflower. A lot of history in this family.

Dan: She took a trip several years ago to England and visited the Mayflower sites, where the ship had left from.

Aaron: After Matt was killed, how did you and Bob meet?

Betty: A girlfriend of mine had a date with a sailor in Newport, Rhode Island, and we went to the Enlisted Club and that's where I met him.

Dan: Was that a dance?

Betty: Yes. I had a car then, I took her up there.

Aaron: What kind of car was it?

Betty: I think it was a Ford. And I had lots of trouble because the guys at the body shop, they thought it was a police car. But anyway, then

I only saw him every couple of weeks. He was going to come back in two weeks, he had every other weekend off, and he didn't show up. So my girlfriend and I went to the beach in Rhode Island two weeks after that, and when I got home, he was there. He came back.

Aaron: And he was in the Army at the time?

Betty: He was in the Marines.

Aaron: Was he at the Chosin Reservoir?

Betty: Yes.

Aaron: Dan, you had said that he was the only survivor of his machine gun platoon?

Dan: Yes, that's what my mother recently told me.

Betty: Yes, and he was shot by our own guns. He had shrapnel wounds. Then he was flown to Japan, and was in the hospital in Japan for I don't know how long. And then they flew him into the Chosin Reservoir. They flew him up there and told him find your way back. And I came to find out one of my elderly neighbors, who's 97, he used to fly troops up there.

Aaron: And he had frozen feet?

Betty: Yes.

Aaron: How did he come to be in the Army?

Betty: We got married the day after he got out of the Marines. He was going to go back to Brooklyn. But we decided, well, we'll just get married. Because I had an apartment in one of those, it was for the veterans, in my hometown; actually it was part of a house, and so we decided just to get married then. And he didn't like living in Rocky Hill. He didn't like living in Connecticut, and he wanted to go back into the service. At one time he talked about going back into the Marines, but we had two kids then — we had Sherry and Dan — plus he joined the Connecticut National Guard and they made him a sergeant, so he went into the Army as a sergeant from the National Guard.

Aaron: Dan, you said yesterday that Bob didn't know his father?

Betty: Right. Well, his father was an alcoholic, and they had really gone down down down once he started drinking. They lived on the third floor over a bar, and he does remember that his mother would send him down to the bar to tell him his lunch was ready. That's all he remembers of his father. And his mother never had one picture of his father.

Aaron: Is it possible that the fact that he grew up without a father figure, or a negative father figure, is what made him a good father to Danny?

Betty: Well, he wasn't really a hands-on father. He was pretty strict. As he got older he got better, but he was strict. I didn't think we were going to make it very long. But we hung in there for 56 years. He liked to be off on his own.

Dan: I remember one of his sayings whenever he'd get really frustrated with something one of the other family members was doing. He'd refer to us as "Youse people." That was a Brooklyn phrase. You remember that, don't you, Mom?

Betty: Yes. We used to tease him about his Brooklyn accent. And he was a little bit jealous that I had been married before.

Aaron: You think so?

Betty: Yes. Because I never talked about Mathew very much. If I'd get mad at him I'd put on my diamond. I think he was a little jealous. He never said he was but he acted like he was.

Aaron: I recently interviewed a woman whose husband was killed in the Battle of the Bulge. She remarried, but she never got over her first husband, and it was a very short marriage. But they didn't have any children. Would you say that you never stopped thinking about Matt?

Betty: Oh no, I always remember our wedding anniversary. I always thought about him. And he was very happy that I was pregnant. First I said I wanted a girl and he said he wanted a boy, and I said, "Okay, I want a boy, too." So that's how I knew what his name was going to be before he was born. And in those days they just put you to sleep. I was sleeping at Hartford Hospital, and they woke me up and said, "Did you know you had your baby?"

"What did I have?"

"A boy."

"Oh, I'm gonna have four more!"

Dan: How did you come to choose my name? Was it after anyone in the family?

Betty: I think he has an uncle Daniel. And my grandfather's Thomas.

Dan: Thomas is my middle name.

Aaron: According to Annabelle Caruso [Mike's widow], she and Mike planned to name their son [who was born six days before Dan] Daniel and Mathew knew that, but he wrote to Mike and said he was going to name his child Daniel if it was a boy. So Mike and Annabelle named their son Larry.

Dan: Afterward, Uncle Bill named his son Dan.

Betty: I don't know, because I never saw them [Mike and Annabelle] after the funeral.

Aaron: Was there any friction between the families? John says your mother didn't like Matt's father.

Betty: Yes. Well, I didn't meet Matt's father until Dan was born. I met him in the hospital. But my mother was the kind of person that if she thinks someone's going to say something bad, she's never going to forget. She'll hold that grudge for no reason at all. So I don't know. Like I said, I never met Mathew's father.

Aaron: What was your wedding like?

Betty: We got married in a Protestant church. Matt came home on leave and we got married. And he was shaking. I started laughing, and my father said to me, "You don't take anything seriously, do you?" Matt told me later that he was shaking because it was not a Catholic church, but he did that because I was pregnant, and he loved me and he wanted to please me. He did ask me to send him a rosary when he was in Korea, and Mother and I went and bought one and sent it to him.

Aaron: Would he have gotten it before he was killed?

Betty: Oh, yes, he got it. Because we got it back. Dan has it now.

Aaron: He said in a letter that he prayed the rosary with Father Griffin in foxholes.

Betty: I sent it to him. John, you probably don't remember, I had the rosary at your father's house after the funeral, and I asked you if you wanted to use it, and you didn't really believe that it was Mathew's. He acted like he didn't believe it and Father Griffin said, "Yes, that was Mathew's."

Aaron: Dan, you spoke yesterday about your earliest memories. Could you go over that again?

Dan: I just said that I don't remember anything before I was probably four and a half, when the funeral was. And I don't remember anything after that for probably another year. I did remember that event with the flag-draped casket and my mother being upset.

Aaron: Do you have any recollection of the Silver Star ceremony?

Dan: No, I don't.

Aaron: But you've read newspaper accounts about it?

Dan: Yes. I was only 14 months old.

Aaron: Tell me about the funeral.

Betty: I don't remember too much about it. I know Father Griffin was there. I remember going to Matt's father's house, and Father Griffin was there, too. We talked, and some of the family was there. Do you remember that, John?

John: The funeral was very large. The Farley-Sullivan Funeral Home handled the remains. It was at St. Augustine Church, which is a large parish in the south end of Hartford. And Monsignor Mulcahy, who was the priest of the church, let the Catholic grammar school out to attend the services, so the whole grammar school was there, too. The church was mobbed, plus Mathew's friends from high school and the neighborhood kids.

Aaron: Now tell me, Dan, you grew up with a father, Bob, who was a little bit jealous of your mom having been married before. How did you learn what you did learn about Mathew?

Dan: I don't remember exactly when I was first told about it, or in my early years, when we talked about that. As I was growing up I always knew, having a different last name, that Bob was my stepfather. And at times I felt that maybe that's what put a little distance between us, and that he knew that I knew he wasn't my real, or biological father anyway. But just our personalities, we didn't have a whole lot in common, and as my mom said, he wasn't a real hands-on father. I don't remember too much of him ever playing ball with me, and then in later years when I was in high school I was in sports, and my mom was working too, full time, and he was in the service, and I know they were busy. But, you know, I never did have a soccer mom. I don't remember them coming to any of my athletic events in high school. Of course when I was a senior in high school my father was in Vietnam. That's when I was really active, in the running for the state championship for the cross country meet in Colorado. It would have been nice to have both parents there.

Aaron: Did you live in Uruguay when he was posted down there?

Dan: No. I started college when he got back from Vietnam. I don't know if there were a few stations in between, but then they were stationed at the Seneca Army Depot in the Finger Lakes region of New York for my freshman year, and a lot of the guys on my dorm floor at Miami were from the Northeast, Pennsylvania, New York, we would all car pool together and pull all-nighters to drive up from Miami. Not car pool, but we'd stuff in the same car sharing the driving, and I surprised her once with one of my friends. We drove to the house at Christmas time, do you reember that?

Betty: Uh-huh.

Dan: I just walked in the door, here I am. I think it was shortly after that, maybe for my last three years of college, that they were in Uruguay.

Betty: He flew down twice to visit.

Aaron: So you basically were on your own?

Dan: Oh, sure. I was very independent. You know, in my opinion, although I was not physically mature because I was a year younger in college, I thought that I was mentally pretty mature and able to be on my own. And I remember, actually, one time when I visited Monsignor Griffin in Phoenix and he made a comment that I could, you know, I was kind of a shy kid, that I could sit down and fit in and have a conversation with younger people, and my peers, or older people.

Betty: I had an uncle, my mother's brother, and he said if he were going to go on a trip into the wilderness, he would like to have Dan with him because Dan was so level headed.

Dan: That's very interesting. I have a couple more comments about that because when I was engaged to my former wife, in Colorado, one of the roommates of my house told Leslie, whom I was engaged to, the exact same thing. I didn't know that, Mom. He said, not that I have any particular wilderness skills, but he told her that if he was stranded on a desert island or out in the wilderness somewhere, that if he had to be with anybody else it would be Dan because he has common sense.

Seventeen, eighteen years later, I was close to the end o my marriage, we were at friends for dinner and I had been applying to the airlines, because I had a lot of flight experience with fixed wing aircraft and helicopters. And our friends told me they'd like to have me as their pilot on an airline because nothing ever bothers you, Dan. Even to this day, people come back from these wars with PTSD and loud sounds bother them. There was a Toyota commercial out a little while ago with all these huge sounds going off and nothing bothers this one guy. I'm like that. When that sound goes off next to me, I don't jump.

Betty: When Dan called and told me that he and Leslie were getting a divorce, I cried.

Dan: We just grew apart over the years. We remain friends today.

Aaron: Did you have children?

Dan: No. We put it off for the first five years, and then, while I was in Okinawa, her parents went through a really bad divorce. And then I think we were just growing used to our lifestyle and for me, it didn't seem to matter whether we had kids nor not. But now in my adult years, now that I haven't had children it's one of my biggest regrets in life, not having children and passing on my genes and my father Mathew's genes, and my mother's. So I choose to think that I'd leave my mark on the world as how I affected other people. I'm not someone who wants a huge building in New York City. I just want to be remembered, and I've told people, to be cremated when I go and be right out there, in that ocean.

Betty: The great Uncle Dan.

Dan: Yes, some of Laurie's kids. I was always in different parts of the country, so I didn't have a lot of interaction with the kids. I regret that sometimes. When I was here around them I should have taken her kids on camping trips and things like that. We're together a lot now, but I tell some people that if I was going to have a headstone, all I would want it to say was "He was a good guy."

Aaron: Tell me about Monsignor Griffin. You went out to visit him two summers. What was he like?

Dan: He was dedicated to his parishes. The first one was in a copper mining town, Clifton, and the second time I went he was on the outskirts of Phoenix, Apache Junction, which at the time was just a short way out in the desert. Now it's swallowed up by the other communities around it. I was talking to Chip [Monsignor Griffin's nephew] yesterday. It was great to see him. I was 15 and he was 10 when we last saw each other, and even though we didn't have a lot of interaction I just remember meeting him when we were out here in San Diego. He said, "Oh yeah, you were always running. You would go out for a run and you wouldn't come back for hours." And I remember in Apache Junction, I would just run along this road out into the desert. I wouldn't see any cars until I got tired and turned around and came back.

Aaron: Did Monsignor ever talk to you about your dad?

Dan: Not much about his personality, just the events that happened. Not in detail, but basically everything that I know now.

Aaron: How did you come to be in the Marines?

Dan: I transferred in the middle of my junior year to Western State College in Gunnison, Colorado. I graduated, and that year I graduated there was bitter cold. Gunnison is known as the coldest spot in the lower 48 states. International Falls in the Midwest claims it at certain times, but they add in the wind chill factor. In Gunnison in the winter it would routinely get to 30 or 40 below zero. And it was funny that when it warmed up to ten degrees above zero, everyone was running around in T-shirts because it was a 40-degree temperature change. But the only way it could get that cold is because it had an inversion. It was set in a small valley. Cold air came off the mountains and sat in that valley. It had to be perfectly still for it to get that cold. On those 30 or 40 below mornings you could walk outside and see the air crystallizing. If any wind was coming at all it would warm up actually, because it would blow the cold air out.

Because it was so cold and I had come to study marine biology, I decided maybe I ought to go back to Miami. So I went back there, enrolled for another semester, and I was only there less than one semester when I decided there's a reason I left there in the first place. I dropped out of that semester and told them I was leaving. I drove up to my grandma's house in Connecticut, got some cold weather clothes I had stored there, and headed back to Colorado. I decided to go back to school there for another year to get my teaching certificate. It was while I was doing my student teaching internship that I happened to wander over to the college campus one day and the Navy recruiters were there. Photography had been a serious hobby of mine. I sat down and talked to them about their photography program, and they said most of the photographers in the Navy are enlisted, and with your college degree you can be an officer. They said "We need pilots right now. If you're interested, you can apply for that." And I thought, well, I loved model airplanes when I was a kid, especially World War II type airplanes, but I never thought I could be a pilot. In our family we never really talked about anything I would do, I mean career goals, so I was on my own about that. I just never dreamed that I could be a pilot myself.

It was getting late in the day, so they took me back to the motel room and sat me down at a desk. I took a three-hour battery of tests and did really well. They got back to me later and said, "You're accepted, but there's a waiting list in the Navy Aviation Officer Candidate program. But if you don't want to wait, the Marines are looking for pilots, too."

I didn't know much about the Marine Corps at the time. I was so naive I didn't even know that they had an air wing in support of the troops. So I wrote to the recruiter in Denver. He sent me all the pamphlets, Wings for the Fleet, training in Pensacola. I said, that looks good to me. So I applied, and called up Monsignor Griffin and told him about it. He ended up getting in touch with a friend of his who was a two- or three-star general, General Kenny Houghton, and he wrote to Monsignor Griffin and said, "He will be in the next class." A few weeks later I was running up hills in Quantico, Virginia, in Officer Candidate School. That's how it happened. It was quite by accident and unexpected, but as we were talking about last night, life takes its turns.

Aaron: And how did you become a rescue pilot?

Dan: My last week in flight school I was awarded the Student of the Week award. I did pretty well once I got into helicopters. I was a natural at it. That's where I wound up, even though when I first applied I was thinking I want to fly jets. Flying helicopters is very difficult to start with, much more than an airplane. You have to be very gentle on the controls. If you over-control the rotors one way, then you over-correct for the other way. It's like a pendulum that gets bigger and bigger. And the instructors bet all the students on their first flights that "We're going to take you out to a football size field and I'll bet you that you can't hover within that." And they were right, because you're used to horsing around an airplane's controls and when you fly a helicopter you rest your forearm so that you're actually not moving with your forearm and you're just gently controlling the controls with just the palm of your hand. And they were right with me, too, and that pendulum gets bigger and bigger, and at some point the instructor says, "Okay, I've got it." But I loved going back there as an instructor myself.

Aaron: Were there any accidents?

Dan: In training, the airplanes and helicopters were on the same field, and occasionally there were some airplane accidents, but mostly just some kind of mechanical failures, or they'd land in farmers' fields. And I remember hearing that the farmers love it because they get to make a claim against the government when an airplane cuts a swath through a little patch of their farm. But there are two squadrons, basic and advanced. While I was in basic training, there were volunteers asked to go search for a Huey which was in the advanced helicopter squadron. On top of the rotor system there's a little bar with weights on the end, 90 degrees out from the position of the rotors, and what that does is, the controls going into the rotors have a tendency of going up and down as they hit the wind, and that weight that's spinning above the rotor acts like a gyroscope and tends to dampen out what the rotors are doing. There was an accident and that stabilizer bar had broken and it hit the rotor. I didn't even know these guys, but there was a one in a thousand chance that that weight would hit the rotor just in a place ... so they said that they probably didn't feel it.

Later, when I was in my squadron here at Camp Pendleton, my squadron actually had some awards for excellent safety records. We set records in several years without any incidents or accidents, so I was lucky that we never lost anybody in our squadron. But I had many, many friends that after they left were killed in various accidents. Even in peacetime. It's a dangerous business.

Aaron: In that accident you were just describing, is it the two pilots who were killed?

Dan: It was an instructor and two students. When I went back as an instructor, I remember there was one airplane crash and some fellow pilots from my squadron were sent out to the scene, to carry the accident investigation team, and the press wanted to just swarm around it and take pictures. Some of the guys in my squadron told them to back off. They had been crawling around the accident site to take pictures of what was a deep smoking hole with the bodies of two Marines somewhere still in it.

But to get back to your question about how I got into search and rescue, after my two years in a combat squadron here at Camp Pendleton, I was stationed at Okinawa for a year. That's when I got to go to the Philippines for jungle survival school, and then Korea for cold weather training. That was on December 6, which was kind of an eerie feeling, the same day my father was killed, that I first flew a helicopter over there.

While I was in Okinawa, I put in for a transfer to C-130s, the big cargo planes. In the Marine Corps their mission is mainly refueling of the jets. But there was a waiting list to get in the Air Force school there. Meanwhile, when I got back to the States I had orders to go to El Toro Search and Rescue. At the time Orange County didn't have their own helicopters, so they had an agreement that they could use us on rescues in the mountains, on the bluffs, when people got into accidents. And my parents lived in Lake Forest when I was stationed there. That's right outside the gates of El Toro Marine Station, and often when we had a mission I could take off in any direction we wanted. We didn't have to go down a runway. So I requested a certain direction which happened to be right over the house, and when they heard me coming they'd go outside and yell and wave at me.

Betty: The first time I heard about twelve helicopters going over my house, I thought, "What in the world's going on?"

Dan: I was doing that for a few months, and that's what I loved doing. I was helping people. A lot of times, if we took an accident victim to Mission Viejo Hospital, which was on my way back to my home in Oceanside, I would stop by the hospital and check up on the people and see how they were doing. I got many letters of thanks from the families of people I had rescued. So by the time the orders came in for me to go to the C-130 squadron, I decided I wanted to stay.

Aaron: Can you describe some of your rescues?

Dan: There were a couple of them. There was a light airplane accident on the other side of the Saddleback Mountains, near Temecula. We got called by the Orange County Fire Department. They had to be on scene first to assess things, and then they would call us. Many times we'd give training lessons, get together with groups of firemen and gather them around helicopters and just familiarize them with how they should operate around a helicopter. Don't get near the tail rotor. When I was an instructor, we had a student in my squadron who got outside to check something and he made the mistake of walking to the back of the aircraft. The tail rotor spins three times faster than the main rotor, so it can be invisible. And this kid got whacked on his helmet by the tail rotor. He was very lucky, he had a crease in his helmet but he wasn't really injured, just surprised and stunned.

So on this particular call, we went out and were directed to the site. Our crewman in the back operated the hoist with one hot mike so he wouldn't have to keep pressing the button to talk to the pilots, because he needs both hands to operate the hoist. So two things he's doing, he's watching our position on the ground and he's giving me very minute corrections, left two feet steady, two feet steady, right two feet steady, and keeping me there. We went to one event in Orange County where we would do a demonstration of a rescue like that. People asked me afterward, "How do you keep it perfectly still?" Well, my skills plus the crewman telling me, constantly, and I'm always shifting my eyes around to different spots on the ground to try to get some reference. So anyway, in the airplane wreck, we rappelled a Navy corpsman down, and sometimes, after we got the victim up in the hoist, if it was critical time-wise we'd leave our corpsman on the ground, zip to the hospital and then come back and pick him up later. But in this case we hoisted him up too. And Orange County was looking for nominees for some kind of humanitarian award, so I put my Navy corpsman in, although he didn't think he was doing anything special, we were just doing our jobs. Somehow the press got hold of it. So I put him in for that award and he ended up getting it.

On another one, we went out at night. It was foggy, and we ended up doing the rescue up on the other side of the hills. And it was so foggy that we couldn't make it back to the base. There were steep ravines, and it just socked in behind us, so we slowed down and just crept along. My co-pilot was calling out my airspeed to me so I wouldn't get too slow or too fast. All of a sudden I saw this one little set of lights. Nobody else knew it but I recognized it. I know where we are. That's a ranch light. So I follow my instincts and get us up and over the mountains and out of the fog, and we ended up taking the accident to Temecula. This was one of those car wrecks, where somebody missed a hairpin turn and went down a steep ravine.

Aaron: This weekend, with the rededication of the chapel, what has that meant to both of you?

Betty: I don't really know how to express myself. I was not here for the original dedication. I felt bad about that. But it's a way to honor him. I've thought a lot of him over the years. I never did forget him, and I'm just happy to be here because I know what sacrifice, he was doing his job, he was thinking about what his duty was, and he was doing his duty. I'm happy to be here. It's a great honor to be here. And to see the family again, that's nice, too, the contact with the Caruso family, and to have Danny, his family, which he hasn't known for years. It's a very nice experience for me.

Dan: I didn't know the Caruso family when I was growing up. This is a great reunion. We maintained contact with the chapel through visits over the years, but this is a really special event, not only because there is a rededication but because of the reunion with the family that I haven't known growing up.

John: It's been a great experience.

Betty: It's such an honor for him. It was his destiny. When my daughter and her husband and I went into the chapel, she said to me, "He's here with us." That's my feeling.

Dan: There have been times in my life where I felt kind of charmed, that I got out of different situations, and felt like I had somebody watching over me, and perhaps it was him.

Aaron: You mentioned yesterday that there was a letter from Matt that you have.

Dan: I think you're talking about a letter that my mom gave to me last year. It's pretty touching that she gave it to me.

Aaron: What was it that he said in the letter?

Betty: He told my parents that I was pregnant, and not to be mad at me, that it was his fault. ... It wasn't his fault. And we were happy that I was pregnant. He was really happy that he was going to be a father.

Dan: It was a lot of writing about their love.

Aaron: What would you like to see in a book about Mathew?

Betty: What kind of a person he was. What he liked and what he didn't like. Sometimes I think about even the way he ate. The special way he ate.

Aaron: How did he eat?

Betty: He never put ketchup on his french fries or anything, and to this day I don't do that either. And when he ate, he ate one thing at a time. He didn't mix what he was eating. And he drank Miller beer. He liked Miller beer. I remember that. It's not much, but that's how it was. And he was really good to me. And he was staying at my mother's house, and my sister in law was pregnant, and I was working. I'd go to work at the Travelers, and he would take Jean to see horror movies. She loved them. So they would go together to the movies. I don't know what movies they were, because I was not interested in seeing anything like that. And everyone liked him. I talked to a cousin of mine recently that John used to know, and she's having mental problems. She doesn't even know who her husband is anymore. "There's a Roger taking care of me, but I don't know why." I said, "Do you remember my first husband?"

She said, "Oh, yes, Mickey. He was so handsome." She remembered. Then she said, "I don't know how I got that up. I don't remember very many things these days." That was just recently. It made me happy when she said that, because she remembered him. He was Mickey. He was always Mickey to me."

Aaron: I thought Mickey was Mike's nickname.

John: I never recall calling Mike Mickey. We used to call him Bud.

Betty: Mike said that Mathew stole his nickname.

Aaron: But he looked up to his big brother, yes?

John: We all did.

Aaron: Dan, what would you like to see in the book?

Dan: A few things. First, probably start with his later years, with his family. His relationship with his brothers, and with me and my mom and our stories, and then of course the incident itself, and the aftermaths, and how it affected both of our families. And then the later things that happen in life in both of our families, and some of your other brothers who joined the Marines, and there's me joining the Marines, and some of the things we did.

Betty: It just came to me – my other ancestor from the Mayflower. Richard Warren. Richard Warren and Isaac Allerton. I couldn't think of his name.

Chaplain Evan Adams. Marine Corps photo by Sgt. Christopher Duncan.

No Greater Love

"Good morning Dan, Elizabeth, Judge" (Evan, the command chaplain, likes to call me "Judge") "William, Captain, Marines, Sailors, ladies and gentlemen. On behalf of the commanding officer, School of Infantry West, Colonel Stefen E. Dien, and the Sergeant Major, School of Infantry West, Sergeant Carlos A. Raina, welcome to the rededication of the Caruso Memorial Chapel."

So began the event we came to California for on June 23, 2014.

"The chapel is named in honor of Marine Sergeant Mathew Caruso, who on 6 December 1950, near the Korean Chosin Reservoir, Sergeant Caruso threw himself in front of enemy gunfire to save the life of the chaplain he was assigned to protect. In August 1953 the United States Marine Corps dedicated this facility in his name.

"The ceremony was conducted then by Lieutenant C.J. Griffin, Chaplain Corps of the United States Navy, the chaplain whose life Sergeant Caruso saved. The bronze plaque located outside the front hatch reads thus: 'To the glory of almighty God, and the memory of Sgt. Mathew Caruso, United States Marine Corps, 7th Marines, 1st Marine Division, killed in action near Koto-ri, Korea, 6 December 1950. The United States Marine Corps humbly dedicates this chapel to his spirit of loyalty, courage and devotion. May it serve to inspire all who enter here to pray. 'Greater love than this no man hath that a man lay down his life for his friends.' St. John, Chapter 15."

The pews were full of Marines. Several dignitaries were supposed to attend, but Camp Pendleton that day was graced with a surprise visit by Dakota Meyer, who only a week before was awarded the Medal of Honor in a ceremony at the White House. Meyer dove on a hand grenade to save the life of his colleagues, and survived, although badly wounded. Ironically, the newspaper coverage of his speech quoted the very same biblical passage that adorns the entrance to the chapel.

There were three speakers at the rededication. At the risk of being slightly redundant, since I was one of them and you already know some of my story, just for the record, I'd like to include their speeches.

"It is my pleasure to now introduce you to three of our special guests," Evan began. "Captain Chip Griffin, Medical Service Corps, United States Navy. Surviving nephew of Chaplain Commander Connie Griffin, United States Navy, whose life was saved as a result of the heroic action in combat by Sergeant Caruso on 6 December 1950 in now what is known as North Korea. Captain Griffin, who lives in San Diego, retired from the Naval Reserve on 1 June 2014 after having served in the Navy for over 27 years. Welcome Captain Griffin.

"Next to him is the Honorable Judge John Caruso, who served in the United States Marine Corps and is a Korean War veteran. The judge attended military training here, at what is now known as SOI West. He is a retired Connecticut Superior Court judge. Welcome Judge.

"Finally it is my pleasure to introduce to you Mr. Dan Caruso, surviving son of Sergeant Mathew Caruso. Dan was born six days after his father, Mathew, was killed in Korea. Dan served in the United States Marine Corps from 1974 to 1985 and was honorably discharged as a captain. Dan received a degree in photography and traveled the West Coast and he currently resides in Oregon on a ten-acre cherry orchard. Ladies and gentlemen, will you please welcome our guests to the stage."

Chip Griffin

Colonel Dien, Sergeant Major Raina, Chaplain Adams, Caruso family, distinguished visitors, sailors and Marines, ladies and gentlemen, it is a singular privilege to be with you today to participate in the rededication of this holy and sacred facility. The circumstances under which this chapel was originally planned, built and dedicated are historic, dramatic, tragic and inspiring. I would like to offer some thoughts and personal memories to this day. I hope they will help round out your perceptions of this chapel and perhaps even serve to enhance its significance to you.

In my family for as long as I can remember the name of Sergeant Mathew Caruso has always been said with reverence, and I'll explain why. In May 1948 my uncle Connie Griffin was ordained as a Roman Catholic priest. Not long thereafter he was commissioned as a lieutenant junior grade in the Chaplain Corps of the United States Navy. At the time, with victory in World War II recently won, it seemed that peace would prevail for many years to come for the United States. But as we all know, such was not the case.

South Koreans refer to the Korean War in much the same way as Americans do to the events of 11 September as 9/11. That is, South Koreans speak of the war that devastated the Korean Peninsula as 6/25 because it was on 25 June, 1950, that the Korean People's Army crossed the 38th Parallel, invading south toward Seoul. On 27 June 1950, President Truman ordered U.S. air and sea forces to support South Korea.

Isn't it striking that the Caruso Memorial Chapel's rededication is happening this week, the very anniversary of the start of the Korean War. The summer of 1950 found Lieutenant j.g. Griffin reporting for duty as chaplain, 2nd Battalion, 7th Marines, here at Camp Pendleton, and deploying with 2-7 to Korea in September 1950.

From my childhood I remember him telling me he had no idea what to expect, except that word was that all U.S. forces would be home by Christmas. The irony of that would become evident in a few months. I do not know the exact circumstances under which my uncle first met then-Corporal Caruso while serving the 2-7, but I do know from my uncle that sincere mutual respect and trust was established between the two men, as they served together those first few months of his deployment. Their bond was ultimately forged under the most difficult of circumstances in the vicinity of a man-made lake called the Chosin Reservoir, not far south of the Chinese border with North Korea. A simple description of the scenario at Chosin as ground combat under frigid conditions in mountainous terrain against a numerically superior enemy does not adequately convey the arduousness or danger of the mission. The strategy and tactics employed during the Chosin Reservoir campaign are a matter of history and examples of bravery from that time are many. However, no act of bravery exceeded that of Mathew Caruso. In that engagement my uncle sustained severe gunshot wounds to the jaw and shoulder and was medically evacuated under combat conditions to Wonsan Harbor, North Korea, from where he was ultimately transferred to the United States for a prolonged period of rehabilitation.

Now, the events of the Chosin Reservoir happened over five years before I was born. My uncle was completely physically rehabilitated by the time I got to know him and he was again serving on active duty. He had a distinguished career subsequent to his service in Korea, serving among other assignments as ship's chaplain on the USS Midway, and chaplain, Naval Air Station Moffett Field. He was medically retired from the Navy as a commander in 1965 following a heart attack. He returned to diocesan priestly duties in the Diocese of Tucson, Arizona, where he retired. He died of natural causes in 1993 at the age of 73.

Being an only child and my father having my uncle as his only sibling, I was very much the center of my uncle's attention growing up. When he judged I was old enough, my uncle told me of his experiences in Korea, of Sergeant Caruso, and of his love for the Navy and the Marine Corps. I know my uncle had a special place in his heart naturally for Dan. It's wonderful to see you again after so many years. We were talking, I think I calculated it's been about 47 years since Dan and I were in the same place at the same time.

My uncle encouraged me to consider a Naval career, and in 1987, at the age of 29, I finally took his advice. I applied for and received a commission as a Navy Reserve officer, another Griffin j.g., this time in the Medical Service Corps. I retired three weeks ago after 27 years of service. How often I thought of the courage and sacrifice of Sergeant Caruso as I served as a sailor. His example of absolute selflessness helped inspire me throughout my career and serves as my inspiration to this day. Sergeant Caruso's actions on 6 December 1950 not only saved my uncle's life, they allowed the furtherance of God's work. I firmly believe this: He, Sergeant Caruso, was the inspiration for my uncle to be a more Christlike servant of God. Before he retired, my uncle led the building up of a parish church in Tucson, Arizona, and establishment of a parish and building of a church in Rio Rico, Arizona. He influenced so many people's lives, bringing them back or closer to God. The effect of Sergeant Caruso's actions have propagated to me and countless others over the years and their benefits are incalculable.

The effects of Sergeant Caruso's actions are not limited to the United States. In 2004, in the course of my military duties, I had a chance to visit the War Memorial in Seoul, South Korea. It's a huge and magnificent museum, constructed mostly of granite and built and operated by the Korean government. Inscribed on the exterior walls are the names of all who died in combat during the Korean War. There you will find the name of Mathew Caruso.

Seeing his name filled me with emotion and the realization of the truly transcendent nature of his service at the Chosin Reservoir. Sergeant Caruso, from the bottom of my heart and on behalf of legions of others who may have ever known your name, I feel your presence. Chaplain Adams, your caring stewardship of the Caruso Memorial Chapel is noteworthy and noble. The reverence my family holds for Sergeant Caruso is matched by the rever3ence you show for his memory, too. And I cannot thank you enough for the invitation to join in the rededication. Thank you, Father."

John Caruso

Good morning. I haven't been back here in quite a while, and Old Smoky looks the same to me. Please don't ask me to climb that mountain again.

I knew we would receive a warm welcome coming here to the chapel for the rededication. And as Aaron and I were driving up here yesterday for an activity, it looked like you'd burned the whole base down as a welcoming ceremony for us [Parts of Camp Pendleton had been severely affected by that summer's brush fires]. I can't believe how much fire damage was out there. Fortunately, it was contained to the brush.

The story of Mathew Caruso is bigger than Mathew Caruso. You've heard the details of his death, which was extremely tragic. But there's a whole family out there that was involved. Some of them are here today, and some of them have passed away. On December 22, 1950, or the

21st, I can't remember, I was home babysitting the kids, and a knock came on the door and I opened it, and it was a telegram from the War Department indicating Mathew was killed in action on December 6th. Keep in mind this was three weeks after he was killed. And the Marines were breaking out of the Chosin Reservoir and we were very hopeful that they were making Wonsan Harbor. And having heard nothing, we were celebrating the birth of Danny and our other nephew, Larry. And Larry became a sergeant major in the Marine Corps.

In the Caruso family we had eight boys and two girls. My oldest brother was 4F, but Mike was a Navy corpsman on Saipan and Tinian and Iwo Jima. He has since passed away. Pat was in the Navy on the USS Midway. He has since passed away. You know about Mathew. I'm still standing as far as I know, and I was lucky seven. The next was Peter, who has since passed away, also a Marine. And Bill, also a Marine, who's with us today with his son Dan. And I have one other brother who was in the Air Force.

When I got the telegram I opened it, and as I said I was home babysitting. My father came home from a carpenters union meeting, and I just handed him the telegram. I couldn't speak. And he absolutely turned white. He was so upset because, I'm not sure of the exact circumstances, but Mathew may have forged his birth certificate and my father found out and still let him leave.

Now, Mathew was due to be discharged in July of 1950. Betty was pregnant with Danny. And the war broke out on June 25, 1950. And Mathew's enlistment was frozen,.

So Mathew, here he is presumably going to be discharged in July, and he's over landing at Inchon. From there they fought all across the Korean Peninsula, and then went by ship up to Wonsan and north towards the Yalu River. And Mathew was ordered to stay back. Father Griffin knew that Betty was going to have a baby. But he refused to stay back. He pleaded with the chaplain.

The rest has already been indicated. But there's some more to the story.

In 1955 I was back here with the 5th Marines, and I received special orders to go to San Francisco. Mathew had been buried in North Korea with 60 other Marines and British commandos in a frozen grave that they had to dig by bulldozer, and there he lay from the day they buried him until 1955.

I received special orders to go to San Francisco and there I met the ship bringing his remains home. And when I first went on the train, a woman walked up to me because I had my uniform on and I had a black armband, and the woman said, "What is the purpose of the black armband?"

I said, "I'm a burial escort."

And she said, "Did you know the Marine that was killed?"

And I said, "Yes. He was my brother."

I could not sit alone on that train. I could not buy a meal on that train. I could not buy a drink on that train. Everybody treated me so well, including people on the platforms as we crossed the country. And we had a full military funeral for Mathew in Hartford, Connecticut. He was laid to rest next to his mother. The sad part is, Matt wrote home after the war broke out, as I was saying, he was due to get out of the Marine Corps in July, because he wanted to go back to school. He needed a job. He had a wife. He had a baby on the way. So my co-author and I said, "Wouldn't it be nice if we went back to his high school, Bulkeley High School in the south end of Hartford, and ask them if they would consider awarding him a posthumous high school diploma? Which is usually not done. It's usually given to returning servicemen or elderly servicemen who'd like to get a GED.

But they had a big ceremony and a big assembly at the high school. It was covered in the local newspapers. They awarded him a high school diploma. And they awarded him something else. They awarded him a cap and gown, which, Betty doesn't know this, but I'm going to give it to her now.

What Evan has done here and what his predecessors have done is just absolutely incredible. To think that I came here in 1952 and it's now 2014. And the work that people have done, the volunteers, the Mormons, as you all know it's a nondenominational chapel, everybody's welcome, and it's on the web site that they were cleaning up the outside of the building, painting the inside. It's a wonderful thing.

Dan Caruso

Good morning fellow Marines, sailors and guests. First of all, I'd like to thank the command for this invitation. My mother and I were not able to make the first dedication. This is very special to us. I also want to thank the chaplain for his tireless dedication for making this happen, and both my uncles Caruso who I didn't know as I was growing up. And Chip, it's nice to see you after all these years. We were five years apart when I first came out here when I was 15 years old. It's nice to see that you carried on the Navy tradition in your family. The Carusos carried on the Marine tradition in ours.

My earliest childhood memory was that flag-draped casket. I was about five years old, and I remember my mother holding me and crying. I don't remember a thing in my life before that. And I remember very little after that for the next year or two. It must have been very traumatic for me to remember that.

About three years before that, I was awarded my father's medal which was pinned on me. I was 14 months old. About that time, my mother married another wonderful man, Robert Smith, who was also a Marine who was at the Chosin Reservoir. He was on a machine gun crew, and as they were battling their way down that narrow corridor, every other member of his crew was killed. He was also wounded. He was patched up, sent back to the line, and walked all the way out of there on frozen feet. He always had problems with his feet. It probably didn't help that when I was a senior in high school he was plodding through the jungles of Vietnam. He provided a wonderful life for us and gave me two great sisters. And he later joined the Army after he was in the National Guard, and served 22 or 23 years and retired as a warrant officer. He passed about five years ago.

We moved all around. I ended up going to four different high schools, and they say it's great for kids to get a great education about the world and about relationships making friends quickly. But it didn't do a lot of good for me about relationships as far as girls were concerned in high school. Twice we moved in the middle of those two school years. Hopefully they have a little more consideration for the kids today.

During the summer between my sophomore and junior year in high school, I had the privilege to come down and visit then Monsignor Griffin, who had a diocese in the small mining town of Clifton, Arizona, a copper mining town. Most of the members of his church were what we now call Hispanic Americans, just wonderful people, and I got to hang out with a couple of boys there, and that's where I first learned the word "Gringo."

We spent a total of six years in Germany beginning in 1955, which was only ten years after the end of World War II. I remember all the bombed out buildings, the scars from all the bullets on the buildings there. The next time I went back I had started junior high school and then high school. We were in Nuremburg, Germany both times, and I remember the massive stadium we called Soldiers Field, the Germans had another name for it but I don't remember. That's the stadium where our high school actually played football, and I started running track there. Through my athletic abilities I was blessed to have the stamina and the endurance and then later the will and determination to become a Marine myself.

I'll backtrack a little bit. On that first visit with Monsignor Griffin, we made a trip out here to San Diego to visit his mother and brother and his brother's son Chip. The three things that impressed me here, first I was a young teenage boy and the song "California Girls" was pretty popular then, and I thought, wow, the Beach Boys were right! The second thing that impressed me was of course the beaches here. The third thing was this incredibly impressive sprawling Marine Corps base. We came to the chapel and that's when I first got to see that beautiful bronze plaque out front. Monsignor Griffin told me at that time that if the Marine Corps ever takes down this building, make sure that you get that plaque. And I thought at the time the Marine Corps is never going to leave here and that plaque will be up here as a tribute not only to my father and Cornelius Griffin but to all Marines who made the same sacrifice.

When I came back in later years as a Marine myself, I did well in flight school and I got my choice of duty stations. Of course I chose Camp Pendleton, and I was stationed at the air wing. We had a lot of various missions. Every time I had a mission that flew over the chapel, or over the hills above, I always pointed out to the different crews and co-pilots that I had, that's my dad's chapel.

I'm very pleased to be here today. When I left here I went to Okinawa, and from Okinawa I went on a cold weather exercise in Korea for a month. And the day that I was actually flying over Korea, in 1978, was December 6, the same day my father was killed. And when we were there I had to fly some missions. We flew out of the Osan Air Force Base out of Seoul, and we had many missions up toward the DMZ, and flying there really brought the message home. It was hard to believe that at the time, just one generation later, the conflict was still there, and now, a generation and a half after that visit, the conflict still exists.

While I was in Korea, for about a month, around Christmastime, they broke us up into groups of four and sent us to Korean families to have a Christmas type dinner. The gentleman whose house we went to was the owner of the local bus lines. While I was there at dinner, I told the story to the gentleman about my father and the Monsignor, and he was very impressed. Before we left, we invited him and his family to join us at the officers club on the night when they also had a USO show. I'd like to share with you something that, he took all our names down, all four of us, and delivered to us a few days later something very special to me. I haven't shared it with too many people but I'd like to share it with you.

For those of you in the back who are unable to see this very well, I'll describe it to you. It's a black lacquered plaque inlaid with mother of pearl, the Korean flag on one side, the American flag on the other, Korean writing on one side, broken English on the other side, and I'll read that to you: "Gratitude Plate, December 19, 1978, First Lt. Daniel Caruso, I express our Sence of gratitude on behalf of Korean Especially. Thank you for your effort you make us live out of danger as you give a precious life and things for Korea or word-peace. For all you Marines that go worldwide and wonder if you're appreciated for your efforts, you are. For those who've tasted freedom, they're thankful to you for your efforts in keeping their freedom."

As far as heroes go, there are many of you in your day to day activities who do heroic things, you're just doing your job. When I left Okinawa I came back and I was assigned to search and rescue Del Toro Marine Base. At the time Orange County didn't have their own helicopter so they had some kind of agreement where they could use us for helicopter rescues. I didn't do normal traffic accidents but we would do things like fly up into the Saddleback Mountains when somebody would miss a hairpin turn on a dark, foggy night, and we'd end up doing a hoist rescue out of there. I'd send our Navy corpsman down to assist the Orange County Fire Department and pull him back up on a hoist with the rotor blades sometimes only feet from the cliffs.

My last duty station was Pensacola, Florida, where I was pleased to be able to share some of my talent and experiences with the next generation of Marine pilots. In your day to day activities, there are things you do just doing your job. When I came back from some of my search and rescue missions I would look down at the little lights of Orange County, and I'd wonder what all those people were doing down there in their houses, and what they'd think if they knew what the Orange County Fire Department and we were doing up there on their part.

I think there was a phrase from Harry Reasoner about heroism, and I'll just do one phrase from it, that as you go about your day to day business there are hours and hours of boredom punctuated by sheer moments of terror. I'm sure you've experienced that, and heroism is just handling day to day jobs in professional fashion backed by great training.

Again I want to thank you for being here today. I just also wanted to say that one day I'll meet my father again, though I've never met him yet, and I like to imagine that it will be like in the movie "Field of Dreams," with him walking out ....

Dan Caruso in 1978

"Someone Watching Over Me"

By Dan Caruso

I do not remember the Silver Star that was pinned over my heart. I do not remember the train trip with my mother to visit Father Griffin at Camp Pendleton where the new chapel was dedicated in my father's name. Nor do I remember anyone from the Caruso side of my family. I was a small child the last time I saw them when Mathew Caruso's body was brought back from Korea and laid to rest. I only remember that flag, and my mom holding me and crying.

My high school summers from 1966 through 1968 always included trips to Arizona to visit with Father Griffin. I came to know him as a man, a priest, a Monsignor passionate for his flocks in his dioceses of Clifton, Apache Junction and Tucson. He very obviously loved Arizona and its people. On that first visit he drove me to San Diego to meet his family and to show me the Caruso Memorial Chapel. I was amazed by that beautiful blue Pacific and the sprawling Marine base on its shores. We came to the remote Camp San Onofre, at the northern end of the base as large as the state of Rhode Island, and there it was, a modest metal building with a sign for the list of services beneath my father's name. This was the spot where the father I never knew helped Father

Griffin construct a makeshift chapel for services in 1950, shortly before they shipped off to Korea. A gleaming white pedestal held the polished bronze plaque with the inscription "Greater Love Hath No Man ..." It looked across to California's golden hills.

Father Griffin was encouraging me to attend the Naval Academy but fate would bring me to marine biology studies at the University of Miami. But my heart was in the Colorado mountains, where I had finished high school, and I transferred to Western State College for my senior year. While interning for a teaching certificate in science, by chance I talked to a pair of Navy recruiting officers who steered me into the Marine Corps flight program. I told Father Griffin and he was excited for me. A short time later he forwarded a letter he had received from an old friend, Kenny Houghton, with a two-star general letterhead. His friend was now the commanding general of the 1st Marine Division and the letter stated that I would be in the next Officer Candidate Class in Quantico, Va. My class saw the arrival of the Marine Corps' 200th birthday.

Because I had been a cross-country runner in high school and college and was in good shape from climbing all over the local mountains, OCS was not a great challenge for me physically. Officers were expected to stay ahead of their troops and that was something I could definitely accomplish. But many of my fellow Marine candidates had a harder time of it. Six weeks after my arrival at Quantico, nearly half of our class dropped on request (DOR). I always tried to help those I could who were having difficulties and probably for that reason was ranked number one in peer evaluations from my platoon mates. After all, we were all in our struggle together and working as a team was the ultimate goal.

After receiving my gold bars I returned on leave to my fiancee, Leslie, in Colorado. Her father, John Towles, had been a Marine aboard the aircraft carrier Saratoga, which had steamed out of Pearl Harbor in November 1941 before the Japanese attack. He shared stories about being a Marine guard for Admirals Fletcher, Halsey and Nimitz, and about the Sara being torpedoed. He later lost a brother in the battle for Peleliu. In 1946 the Saratoga was sunk in the atomic bomb test at Bikini Atoll and is now the best diving attraction there.

John still fit into his dress blues and broke them out so we could take pictures of the two of us together in our uniforms. I still have the

Marine dress blues my father Mathew had worn and John's were battle tested. I felt I hadn't done much yet to deserve wearing my new set of blues, but 11 subsequent years as a Marine would certainly qualify. Just as all enlisted Marines were qualified as riflemen, including the cooks and clerks, all Marine officers are qualified to lead a platoon in combat, including aviators and even the lawyers. So what followed was another six months of infantry officer training in Quantico at what is known as "The Basic School." There were no longer any "90-day wonders." We would all become 90-day plus six month wonders.

Flight school in Pensacola was known as the "pressure cooker." The goal was to weed out those who could not handle performing the duties of flying an aircraft under stressful situations. For the Navy Captain commanding our Aviation Training Wing, it was also a numbers game. He was assigned a quota of graduates for the year. If that projection fell behind, then a normally 12-month program was squeezed into 10 months for new check-ins such as myself, with no reduction in the requirements to complete all the flights and ground school courses. The pressure was really on.

I was hoping to fly jets, but instead ended up in the helicopter pipeline. It was like a charm. I instantly knew that's where I belonged and I was a natural at it. In later years, whenever I was able to give helicopter rides to my fellow trainees who did end up flying jets, the typical response was, "Wow, I've been missing this all these years?" When I received my wings, the presiding officer was Rear Admiral Burt Shepherd. After hearing his biography, Leslie and I introduced ourselves as fellow Western State College graduates. We later received a very nice letter, this time on letterhead with two gold stars on a blue flag, from him wishing us the best. We sent a photo of all of us together to the alumni association, which published it in their newsletter.

Since I ranked high in my graduating class, I had my choice of duty stations. Camp Pendleton was the obvious choice for me. I arrived at my squadron just as the older single engine Hueys, many of which still had bullet hole patches from their service in Vietnam, were being replaced by the larger, more powerful twin engine Hueys. Many of my squadron mates had flown the old birds over there. One of my mates, now retired Lt. Col. Dave Mirra, has a son who also joined the Marines, went to flight school and was assigned to the very same squadron, likely flying the very same aircraft his dad and I flew. His son has now seen the

Marines transition into even more powerful Huey helicopters. On one mission, Dave and I were piloting as a film crew focused on telling the story of our crew chief. Soon we were surprised to see part of that film used in a Marine Corps recruiting ad shown during the NFL playoffs.

I loved the varied missions of the all-purpose Hueys, from troop and cargo carrying, to resupply, recon inserts, parachute drops and medevac. Our missions took me daily all over Camp Pendleton and to ships operating off the coast. Whenever we passed by the newly built San Onofre nuclear power plant we would joke about getting our "morning glow." On one mission I picked up a recon team and its lieutenant, only to find out that the lieutenant was another Western State graduate, Chuck Cligget, and I remembered having played intramural basketball against him. After the Marines, Chuck went to law school and returned to our college town of Gunnison, Colo. On that mission we took a photo which also ended up in the alumni newsletter. Many of my missions carried me directly over the chapel or into the hills above it. I was always proud to point it out to my various crews.

During my second year at Camp Pendleton I was introduced to Gunnery Sgt. Dub Allen, who worked for the Pendleton Scout, the base newspaper. He wanted to do a story about me visiting the chapel. I told him to write to my grandma in Rocky Hill, who had the original photos of the first chapel dedication and of my father Mathew together with Chaplain Griffin in Korea. The photo of the Silver Star being pinned on me was there, too. I was expecting a short article with a few pictures but when it was published it covered a full page, to my surprise. A condensed version made it into Leatherneck Magazine and Father Griffin contacted me to tell me he had seen it. A copy of the Scout article remains in the chapel entrance today. The last sentence reads, "1st Lt. Caruso will always have an attachment to Camp Pendleton, probably greater than any other Marine ... part of his family is here."

While the Huey squadrons in Hawaii boarded the fleet for Pacific cruises, the West Coast squadrons remained land-based, with individual pilots rotated to year-long unaccompanied tours with the combined Huey/Cobra squadron in Okinawa. The other helicopter squadrons, those with wheels on their aircraft, called us "skid kids," a nickname we proudly wore. Beautiful coral-laden tropical waters stretched below me on flying days in Okinawa. A World War II history buff, I was fascinated by all the historical sites of the battle we overflew.

When winter came a number of our aircraft and crews were sent to Korea for cold weather exercises. I found myself flying over the Sea of Japan toward the Korean Peninsula on Dec. 6, 1978, 28 years to the day that my 19-year-old father was killed at the Chosin Reservoir. An eerie feeling enveloped me. We operated out of Suwon, Korea Air Force Base along with elements from an H-46 Sea Knight squadron. The Koreans had constructed an intense anti-aircraft perimeter around Seoul following the strafing of the presidential palace the year before, when a South Korean defector wanted to make his parting statement from an armed plane. While transiting that perimeter I often thought of the Marines battling their way inland from the Inchon landing in fierce house-to-house fighting, my father and Chaplain Griffin right along with them, 28 years earlier. After passing the ROK and U.S. Army camps up toward the DMZ, large inverted T's were visible in a line on the ground to help prevent pilots from accidentally wandering across. A month before, a team of North Korean infiltrators had tunneled under the DMZ and killed a number of ROK troops before they were stopped.

On the return trip to Okinawa the flight of four Hueys I was in had to divert to Taegu Air Force Base because of bad weather. As we parked on the flight line, because we had come in with such short notice, a platoon of Korean soldiers surrounded our clearly marked Marine helicopters. They aimed in, locked and loaded, until they could be sure it wasn't a North Korean trick. I was impressed how calmly our crew chiefs went about their post-flight engine checks before we shut down the aircraft. Major incursions still occur today, 64 years since the Marines fought their way down out of the frozen Chosin. The South Koreans are still deadly serious about their security from their neighbors to the north.

On another mission to Korea, after we landed, we discovered a bent bolt in the flight control linkage to the main rotors. The Army helicopter mechanics who helped us take it apart estimated that the bolt would not have lasted another hour before it failed. There have been many instances in my life, both in flying and in my civilian life, when I have had similar very close calls. But I always felt that someone was watching over me. I have a feeling that someone is the father I never met, Mathew Caruso.

On another occasion, we had flown a number of our squadron aircraft from Camp Pendleton to Marine Corps Base Twentynine Palms to participate in Brave Shield, a huge combined Army, Air Force and

Marine exercise. On one mission I was assigned to pick up two lieutenant colonels. They had lost contact with one of their units and personally wanted to find them. Small camps of Marines were scattered all over the desert. We were having no luck hopping from one camp to another attempting to find the "lost" unit.

We circled one larger camp in preparation for landing. It had a designated zone covered by a large flexible fiberglass mat big enough to land two Hueys on while keeping the dust beneath in place. Those mats are designed to be held in place with pegs, but as we made our approach no one in the camp came over the radio to tell us that they were breaking camp. The pegs had been removed. On our short final approach, while we were still about 30 to 40 feet above the ground, it happened in a sudden "Whoosh!" In the span of two seconds, the entire mat rose in front and above us, covering the whole of the sky directly in front of me. It was a great looming monster before us. My instincts took over. My Huey was no longer a flying machine that I was operating; it was a part of my being, an extension of my own body that would instantly react to what my arms and legs were doing. I flipped the bird on its side, now facing 90 degrees from our direction of flight. With the doors pinned open in the back, the view those lieutenant colonels and my crew chief got went instantly from a pleasant view of the camp to a face-down view of the desert floor. Simultaneously I had yanked the collective control all the way up to my armpit for maximum power. The result was that the entire rotor disc, now turned sideways to the giant curtain, acted like an enormous fan and blew the mat away from us, clear of any danger. I flipped the bird back over and gently put her down on the desert floor. She had saved us.

Had we been in one of the older single-engine Hueys, the results would have been very different. When I yanked all that power to stop our forward motion I had likely over-torqued the transmission. I had been a little too occupied in the moment to see what the gauge was registering, so we waited for a maintenance team to inspect it to clear us to fly back to our staging area. I remember my crew chief, Corporal T.J. Price, telling me, "Lieutenant, if we had gone any farther forward than when you first saw that thing, it would have swallowed us up." There is no doubt in my mind that my instincts and quick reaction saved the aircraft and everyone aboard. That's the kind of action deserving of an air medal. But when we returned to my squadron at Camp Pendleton, not a word was ever said about the incident or my flying skills. But my crew knew, and that's all that really mattered. Someone was definitely watching over us on that day.

Interestingly, two other incidents occurred within a mile of the chapel. On the hill above, a landing zone director put me down on an old rusty metal fencepost not visible to anyone in the tall, dry grass. It punctured the skin of the helicopter but missed all vital parts. And a wingman flying a second bird clipped a power line that luckily broke just above the skids. In later years I would lose many friends who weren't so lucky in helicopter accidents all around the world, from the Southern California deserts to the Alps of France, the waters off Norway, and a valley in Japan.

When my year on Okinawa ended, I received orders to become a Search and Rescue pilot at El Toro Marine Corps Air Station in Orange County, Calif. Medevac had always been one of my favorite missions, and doing it full time for the next three years was an incredibly rewarding experience. We worked hand in hand with the Orange County Fire Department whenever an accident scene they were called to required the use of an airborne hoist. Hairpin turns in the Saddleback Mountains are very dangerous for vehicles on dark, foggy nights. We also took diving accident victims 26 miles across the sea to Santa Catalina, where USC operated a hyperbaric chamber. One of our oddest rescues involved picking up some anti-venom serum to deliver for a snakebite victim. We operated single pilot during the day, so I often filled the co-pilot's seat with a crew chief or Navy corpsman and often gave them a little stick time. I thought it was a good idea to give them the basics of at least being able to land the helicopter should anything happen to me while airborne. One of those corpsmen, Petty Officer Don Willey, decided to apply to the Army Warrant Officer flight program. When I checked into my next duty station as a flight instructor in Pensacola, where all Navy, Marine and Coast Guard student aviators are trained, I received an invitation to attend the new Warrant Officer Willey's flight school graduation in nearby Fort Rucker, Ala.

The graduation ceremony and reception afterward was a dress blues affair. The only Marine in attendance, I was feeling pretty darned spiffy and even got a few admiring glances from some of the ladies. Army dress blues are nice but they just didn't compare. That is, until I met an older gentleman in his Army blues who really knew how to dress his up.

I do not recall his rank because I was intensely focused on the light blue ribbon with the tiny white stars holding a medallion worn around his neck. I had never seen one before. I was instantly humbled and in awe of this Medal of Honor winner.

My very first duty in the advanced helicopter squadron was to fly down to Key West and meet with the officers of the USS Lexington operating off the island. Because of a mechanical limitation discovered in the older Hueys, my squadron had not "hit the boat" for carrier qualifications in a couple of years. But now that limitation was mechanically resolved and I served as liaison for the Lady Lex's crew who were not used to operating with flights of training helicopters. Forty miles off the coast of Pensacola, Lady Lex's home port, it was a beautiful sight to see my squadron's Hueys arriving overhead.

When I arrived back at the squadron I was assigned as the tactics flight leader. In addition to scheduling all the flights for 25 students in their final stage of helicopter training and a dozen flight instructors, I flew nearly as much as all of them. One exception, however, was Navy Lt. Dan Hansen, nicknamed Grizz. A fellow Coloradoan, Grizz sported a beard in those days of Admiral Zumwalt's return to the age-old Navy tradition allowing them. Grizz was on track for and finally did break the Navy Training Command record for instructional flight hours, logging nearly 1,000, which was the maximum that could be flown in a year under crew rest rules.

The students in my flight were required to check off whether they had completed a scheduled flight. Those who failed that simple task were dinged a "beer frame," a six-pack of beer payable to the flight upon graduation and receipt of their golden Naval Aviator wings. Some forgetful students ended up owing cases, all of which ended up buried in a two foot deep hole on Pensacola Beach's white sands and packed with ice during our periodic flight parties, all students, instructors and families invited. My students were always appreciative that we always upheld our promised graduation date, even if we had to make the extra effort to fly around bad weather that frequently rolled across the Gulf Coast. We always kept their firm date so that out of town family could attend their winging ceremony.

During the rescue mission in Grenada a number of Cobra pilots were killed. There was a call for replacement pilots and our squadron representative at the Wing HQ volunteered. I was bumped up to his job as senior standardization officer, who gave the squadron instructor pilots their check rides. One of the weekly national news magazines was being passed around. It contained a large photo of the bodies of some of those Marine Cobra pilots washed up on Grenada's shore. To put it mildly, we were all pissed that the magazine could be so incredibly insensitive to the families of those Marines.

I often volunteered my weekend time by instructing instrument navigation flights, eight flights in one weekend. When we arrived in Corpus Christi one weekend, my students took me out to town to a local bar known for its Kamikazes. We toasted the Marines in Lebanon and the Marines in Grenada no longer with us. I still have the certificate from the bar qualifying me as a Kamikaze pilot. That reminds me of a joke I heard on the radio five decades ago. It was an ad for a Kamikaze, used only once. Shades of Okinawa past!

During my time in Pensacola, the Vietnam era Hueys were being replaced by smaller Bell Jet Rangers for fuel savings. They were being flown to the mothball fleet at Davis Monthan Air Force Base. I was sitting in a Jet Ranger on the flight line one morning readying for a flight with my two students when the last of the Hueys taxied out to leave for Arizona. The radio crackled and I recognized the voice of my squadron commander, Lt. Col. Tom McDonald. "Hueys departing after twenty years of faithful service." There could not have been a more fitting tribute to the workhorse helicopter of my generation.

In the spring of 2014 my mother visited the chapel with my sister Sherry, who had never before seen it, along with Sherry's husband, Tony. I was where you can usually find me these days, working outdoors on my ten-acre cherry orchard in northwestern Oregon, when the call came. There was going to be a rededication of the chapel. I had first come to this wine country region of the Willamette Valley nearly 20 years before to look up an old squadron mate at Camp Pendleton, retired Lt. Col. Doug Davis, and his wife, Jane. They had purchased an old abandoned dairy farm on just over a hundred acres with beautiful barns built from huge timbers. Doug was still flying helicopters with a couple of local companies and leased his land to local farmers. I immediately fell in love with the area. Each year as I traveled through with my RV and my cameras, the Davises were incredibly generous, allowing me to stay on their farm for short visits. While at Camp Pendleton Doug and Jane adopted two baby boys from Korea who had grown to be fine young men. Each year Doug would keep me informed about other squadron mates who were recently lost to accidents or illnesses. And sitting at his picnic table outside the farmhouse, we lifted our beers to them in memory.

Throughout my adult life I had stopped by the chapel on numerous occasions, but the next time would be something special. While coordinating with Chaplain Evan Adams, I found out that my Caruso uncles John and Bill would be there along with Bill's son Dan. I had met his other son, Anthony, after my Aunt Jean had reached out to me on Facebook. Anthony's arranging of a surprise visit for his folks to see me at my home was a special event. I had not seen anyone from that side of my family in sixty years. And now through Facebook I am in contact with a number of my cousins back East. I was also pleased to hear that Chip Griffin would be at the rededication.

On a glorious Southern California June morning my mom and I met the Caruso family at the chapel. Also there was a Russell cousin's daughter and her Marine husband stationed very close to the chapel. My mom was wearing a cameo necklace that my father had given her 63 years earlier when he had returned from his Mediterranean cruise. The chapel was packed with Marines and Sailors. Months earlier I had read a newspaper article about the Church of Latter Day Saints' efforts to refurbish the chapel with help from generous donations from local businesses and volunteer work from individual Marines. Now I would be able to thank them all in person. On this day the chapel had never looked so good. It had come a long way since that day when my father put together some crates for Father Griffin. So many people have contributed to the Caruso Memorial Chapel. Chaplain Evan Adams has dedicated himself to keeping its story alive by ensuring every new Marine infantryman at San Onofre hears it from the annals of Marine Corps history. His dedication to those Marines is inspiring.

The atmosphere that day was both solemn and electric. When Chip Griffin and my uncle John Caruso gave their talks during the dedication I learned some things about Chaplain Griffin and Mathew Caruso I had not known before. When John relayed the story of his burial escort you could hear a pin drop. I was emotionally choked up and wondered if I could make it through my talk. I don't think there was a dry eye in the chapel. The presentation of his brother's recently awarded high school cap and gown to my mom was both thoughtful and touching. I finally got composed and was proud to show the Silver Star pinned on me as a baby and the plaque given to me by a Korean businessman, thanking me for the sacrifice for the people of Korea.

Afterward the commanding officer of the Infantry Training Battalion, Colonel Stefan Dien, presented each of the speakers with a beautiful framed photo of the chapel as it stands today and his unit's challenge coin, both of which I shall treasure and add to what we called "I love me" walls, places where mementos are displayed — photos, plaques and awards. Mine also contains my Marine officer's sword, flight helmets and a tail rotor blade from one of the Hueys I flew, presented to me by my crew chiefs. With each passing Marine Corps birthday and Veterans Day I am proud to have served and appreciate all the other veterans who have done their part.

Chaplain Adams concluded the rededication. Another Silver Star winner approached me and pressed a dogtag into my palm. On one side stands the U.S. Marine Corps emblem. The reverse inscription reads:

"I will be strong and courageous.
"I will not be terrified or discouraged,
"for the Lord my God is with me
"wherever I go."

I now carry that tag in my wallet wherever I go. A woman came up to me before we left the chapel and said she liked that I kept my father's Silver Star in my left breast pocket, close to my heart. There has been talk of upgrading his medal to the one with the light blue ribbon with the tiny white stars. That would be wonderful; his actions certainly deserve it. But for me an upgraded medal would not mean as much as that Silver Star pinned on me all those years ago for what Sgt. Mathew Caruso and Chaplain Griffin did.

And what better memorial could one person, one Marine have? A chapel that stands as a tribute to all those heroic deeds by Marines, past, present and future who have made, and will continue to make, that sacrifice, and to all those whose stories have never been told.

- - -

Acknowledgments

This book would not have been possible without a team behind it. Special thanks to Jeff and Patty Lee, who organized the very successful First Annual Mathew Caruso Memorial Scholarship Golf Tournament; Marine Corps veteran Jerry Howard, Rev. John Mitner and Al Nweeia for their role in the ongoing effort to have Mathew's Silver Star upgraded to the Medal of Honor; Gary Roy and Marianne Mihalyo of the Iwo Jima Memorial Historical Foundation for their encouragement and support; U.S. Navy Lieutenant Commander Evan Adams for his phenomenal work in making sure the Marines who worship at the Caruso Memorial Chapel at Camp Pendleton know the story of its namesake; Jerry Longo of the Connecticut State Police Alumni Association for allowing me to tell Mathew's story at one of their events; Dan Caruso and Betty Smith, Mathew's son and widow, for sharing their stories; Dan's cousin Larry Caruso, who was born the day Mathew was killed, and who contacted Connell Maguire after reading his story about Mathew on the Internet; Larry's late father, my older brother, Mike Caruso, who was a Navy corpsman on Iwo Jima, for inspiring both Mathew and me and others in my family to join the Marines; Mike's widow, Annabelle Caruso, for sharing her story along with a wealth of photos and newspaper articles; The Chosin Few, the Korean War Project, and the U.S. Navy Chaplain School for the wealth of information about the "Forgotten War" they have preserved; authors Eric Hammel, Donald Knox and James Brady, among others, for first detailing some of the accounts in this book; Stanley Modrak and Joe Hendron for sharing their first person accounts.

Thanks also to Deborah Rothstein and Jennyfer Holmes of the Hartford Foundation for Public Giving for their guidance in establishing the Mathew Caruso Memorial Scholarship Fund; my little brother Billy and his son Dan Caruso, who met his cousin Dan for the first time at the chapel rededication in June of 2014; Marine Sgt. Christopher Duncan for his great photos and for covering the chapel rededication when a major event was happening at the other end of Camp Pendleton;

and, speaking of Duncan, the crew at the Dunkin' Donuts on Main Street in Avon where my co-author and I met every Thursday for almost two years when we weren't meeting at Luke's Donuts; Bulkeley High School Principal Gayle Allen-Greene for her enthusiasm in awarding Mathew a posthumous diploma; Nanette Levin of the Avon Chamber of Commerce for her help with graphics; my children, Amy Gay, Jessica Byrd, Jason Caruso, Rick Minnich, Valerie Bischof and Heather Coghill for their support; my Golden Retriever Cooper and my Maine Coons Oliver and the late Tucker for their companionship and inspiration, and my wife, Marilyn, for understanding and putting up with me while I pursued this project.

– John Caruso

Korean War sources

The Korean War Project (koreanwar.org)
Chosin: Heroic Ordeal of the Korean War, by Eric Hammel
The Korean War, an Oral History, by Donald Knox
Why Marines Fight, by James Brady
Hostage of the Mind, by Stanley Modrak

Other books by Aaron Elson

Tanks for the Memories
A Mile in Their Shoes: Conversations With Veterans of WWII
The Armored Fist: The 712th Tank Battalion in World War II
Nine Lives: An Oral History
They Were All Young Kids

www.semperfi-padre.org

A portion of the proceeds from the sale of this book will go to support the Mathew Caruso Memorial Scholarship Fund. To make an additional donation, go to www.hfpg.org/donate/ and enter Caruso in the search bar.